BARBARA SMITH

HOUNSLOW

Ghost Stories of Alberta

Copyright © 1993 by Barbara Smith

ISBN 0-88882-152-2

Hounslow Press
A member of the Dundurn Group

Publisher: Anthony Hawke
Editor: Dennis Mills
Designer: Gerard Williams
Compositor: Robin Brass Studio
Printer: Transcontinental Printing Inc.

Front Cover Photograph: Gerard Williams
Interior Photographs: Robert and Barbara Smith except McKay Avenue School (Chapter 1) by Barry Hunter

Publication was assisted by the **Canada Council**, the **Book Publishing Industry Development Program** of the Department of **Canadian Heritage**, the **Ontario Arts Council**, and the **Ontario Publishing Centre** of the **Ontario Ministry of Culture, Tourism and Recreation.**

Care has been taken to trace the ownership of copyright material used in this book. The author and the publisher welcome any information enabling them to rectify any references or credit in subsequent editions.

Second Printing: July 1993, Third Printing: March 1994, Fourth Printing: March 1995, Fifth Printing: January 1997, Sixth Printing: August 1998, Seventh Printing: July 1999. Printed and bound in Canada

Hounslow Press
8 Market Street
Suite 200
Toronto, Ontario, Canada
M5E 1M6

Hounslow Press
73 Lime Walk
Headington, Oxford
England
OX3 7AD

Hounslow Press
2250 Military Road
Tonawanda, NY
U.S.A. 14150

For Bob, Debbie, and Robyn.
Your love, support and unfailing good humour
make everything possible;
I cannot imagine my world without you in it.

Contents

Acknowledgments

While compiling this collection of stories I have been privileged to meet some truly extraordinary people. Leads for new tales have come from completely unexpected sources. Friends, acquaintances, and total strangers have kept my project in mind as they went about their own lives. If they heard something that even resembled a ghost story, they called me. This book would be missing some unique tales, were it not for these thoughtful people. Some have asked to remain anonymous. I shall respect that wish and only add my sincere thanks.

I would like to publicly acknowledge all of the others who have been so helpful. They include, Myca Belle of Calgary; Kevin Blades, editor of *Canadian Emergency News*; Tony Cashman, Edmonton historian; Betty Ann Coddere, editor of *Teaching Today*; Brian Dunsmore of CKUA; Jean Frances of Fort McMurray; Dr. George Fritz, professor at the University of Calgary; Lena Goon, Whyte Museum, Banff; Kerklan Hilton, communications coordinator at Fort Calgary; Angela Jones, Special Collections Library, University of Alberta; Al Kachur of Camrose; Mike Kostek of Edmonton Public Schools; Denise Lyons of Edmonton; Craig McLeod of Edmonton; Dr. Bill Meilen, professor at the University of Alberta; Jack Peach, Calgary historian; Frank Silliker, president, Calgary Fire Department Museum Society; Rick Smith, Heritage Park, Calgary; Martin Stanley of Victoria; Deborah Trumbley of Calgary; the staff at the Calgary Public Library; and the staff at the City of Calgary Archives.

If I have forgotten anyone, I apologize. The omission, you can be sure, has not been caused by any lack of gratitude, just bad record keeping.

There are two people who deserve very special thanks. Ron Hlady and Dianne Harris went out of their way on numerous occasions to track down potential stories for me. There was a time when my phone would ring and I assumed it would be Ron with another name and phone number for me. If a lengthy fax began to unroll, it was probably Dianne sending some more nuggets my way. To both of you my sincere thanks. Your help was invaluable and your efforts appreciated.

A warm thank you also goes to Tony Hawke of Hounslow Press – your enthusiasm and support are much appreciated – and to my helpful editor, Dennis Mills.

*   *   *

For my grandchildren and their peers – who will need trees as much as books – arrangements have been made to plant a sufficient number of trees to compensate for those used in publishing this volume.

Introduction

People frequently ask me why I would tackle a project like this. They expect to hear about my haunting experiences, or that I am psychic. Unfortunately, I have to disappoint these questioners. When I started this collection, I don't think I even believed in ghosts. My original motivation was intrigue. I love a mystery.

Since my investigations began, however, I have had experiences that I cannot explain. The first occurred in Edmonton's McKay Avenue School. Ron Hlady (one of my sources) and I had invited psychics Blanche Moskovici and Byron Thompson to tour the school and discuss their findings with us. We were the only people in the school at the time and the four of us were together during the entire visit. We left a room in the 1912 addition after a fairly careful examination of it. Twenty minutes later we returned to the room. Ron glanced to the far corner and noticed that the file cabinet drawers were open. All of us agreed that those drawers had been closed when we'd been in the room only minutes before.

That particular incident didn't really disturb me; I invented some excuse for it. But on an afternoon I had purposely cleared to devote to this manuscript, an incident occurred for which no such excuse was possible.

After going to my basement office and turning on the computer, I realized I must have left my glasses upstairs, where I'd been reading the newspaper. But they weren't there. After wasting nearly an hour searching for them, I gave up in frustration and set to work without them. Predictably, I only lasted a couple of hours before eye strain forced me to give up the work. To ease my headache, I took my dog for a walk. When I returned, something made me check my briefcase. To this day, I deny putting my glasses there. I was the only one in the house – I thought.

Early in my research for out-of-town stories, I spoke at length with some of the staff at Heritage Park in Calgary. About a week later I needed to refer to the notes I'd taken during the phone conversation. The steno pad I'd been using was nowhere to be found. I tore the house apart looking for it, even though I remembered having put the pad away in the desk I was at while talking on the phone.

That evening I explained my dilemma to my husband, who presumed that in my panic to find the notes I'd not done an organized search. Drawer by drawer, he systematically took everything out of the desk. The steno pad was not there. I had no choice but to swallow my pride and phone Heritage Park for a second time. I did this and then followed the call up with a day-long visit to the Park. By this time I had so much additional information and such a feeling for the haunted buildings in the Park that I was not the least bit concerned about having lost my original notes. However, the next morning, when I opened the desk drawer, the pad was the first thing I saw. When I told this to my husband, he stared blankly at me for a moment and then shook his head, "It certainly wasn't there when I looked for it" was all he would say about the matter.

Undoubtedly, the strangest occurrence took place in early May 1992. Edmonton weather usually shows off its every variation during this month, and 1992 proved no exception. I had set aside a particular day to work solidly on the research material I'd collected. At about 11:30 a.m., I stopped working for an early lunch. I was not really hungry but I was extremely cold. I only took about twenty minutes for a break because the kitchen was quite warm and I was soon comfortable again.

My writing was going extremely well that day and I was quite pleased with the amount of work I was getting done. Despite this, I felt very cold again shortly after my lunch break. Not wanting to stop production, I put a sweat shirt over the long-sleeve T-shirt I'd been wearing. This did help, but my concentration was soon being affected by cold hands and feet.

There wasn't much I could do about my nearly numb fingers; I needed them to type. But I did put on a pair of woollen work socks, over my regular socks, and resumed working. Several hours and a great deal of work later, I turned off the computer. I was glad to get out of the cold basement.

Minutes later, my younger daughter drove up. She was wearing shorts, a sleeveless T-shirt, and asking for a cold drink. I still had not warmed up enough to take off any of my extra clothes. We made quite a pair standing there, staring at each other. It was clear that my daughter was the one who was dressed for the weather: the forecasters had predicted a high of 29 degrees C and it had certainly reached that.

To explain myself and my strange attire, I asked my daughter to come down to the office with me. Admittedly, basements are usually cooler than the rest of a house, but what we discovered was not "normal." My office is adjacent to the recreation room, and I'd been working with the office door open. The recreation room was its usual cool space, but as soon as we stepped through the doorway into the office we could feel a dramatic drop in temperature. We stepped back and forth through the threshold several times, fascinated with the phenomenon.

Feeling a bit strange about staying in the house under these conditions, we decided to go to our favourite coffee shop. When we returned, the temperature of the office was identical to that of the rest of the basement. Thankfully, whatever negative energy I'd attracted that afternoon had left and there's never been another such occurrence.

Other disappearances happened during my research, and I was dismayed because it was ghost stories, good ghost stories, that vanished.

The progress of collecting stories was frustrated for various reasons. Sometimes people changed their minds about talking to me. If the tales were very personal, that was understandable. Such was the case of the woman from the south of Alberta whose deceased son has visited her over the years. The special twist to this one was that the son's ghost was aging over the years, just as he would have done in life.

Years ago, I was told by a young man employed at a chronic care hospital that the basement of that venerable old building was haunted. Having walked through the tunnels there myself, I could certainly attest to its spookiness. The place has been torn down now; the young man has gone where all good Albertans want to go – British Columbia; so little can be done to investigate the story.

The evening we were having the conversation he explained that he couldn't talk to me officially without the permission of hospital administrators. But I was still interested.

It seemed that years ago a middle-aged woman who had been employed in the housekeeping department of the hospital had died. Scuttlebutt had it that the cleaner liked young men and took advantage of her supervisory position to have her way with more than a few.

"I don't know whether that's true or not," my confidant concluded. "I just know I always feel as though there is someone watching me when I'm down there. It makes me feel very uncomfortable and I'm always relieved to get back upstairs."

An employee of another old, chronic care hospital, this one still standing, said that the school building on the grounds is commonly accepted as being haunted. Again, the basement area is apparently home to ghostly activity. Despite tenacious snooping, I couldn't turn up anything more concrete about either haunted hospital.

Attempting to investigate the ghosts at the Provincial Museum was, perhaps, my most frustrating research experience. Different people gave me tantalizing tidbits of information about the Museum, the Archives, and even Government House, which sits on the same exquisitely landscaped grounds.

"There's an old guy who sits at a map-table poring over documents at night, long after the archives is closed," I was told by one source.

"The storage rooms in the museum are really haunted," said another.

"There are displays that natives won't go near," someone else told me. "They're just too spooked by the spirits around the setting."

Sadly, unscrupulous journalists had misquoted and distorted some of the stories that the museum staff had shared. As a result, they were not cooperative about talking to me.

Some ghost stories have been concocted for a particular purpose. Unfortunately, after the story of the ghost at the Legislature Building fulfilled its purpose, the legend persisted. I had never heard the tale before it was mentioned to me by the owner of a used book store. He said he remembered hearing somewhere that "the 'Ledge' is haunted." This was an exciting find. If I could get this one for the book, it would erase the pain of having the Provincial Museum ghosts slip through my grasp.

The next morning I was at the library in the Legislature, bright and early. The first person I asked looked shocked by my question. She referred me to a gentleman who kindly brought me a file-folder of newspaper clippings and a very impressive looking, hard-cover book entitled *The Alberta Legislature: A Celebration.* A tantalizing reference to the ghost indicated that the Carillon Room is thought by some to be haunted. I noted the author's name and called him later the same day.

Frank Dolphin chuckled when I told him the nature of my call but said he had no further information than what he'd included in the book. He suggested I contact Oscar Lacombe, Alberta's Sergeant-At-Arms.

Feeling hot on the trail of a real coup, I placed the call immediately. Mr. Lacombe tried to downplay the ghost story, but by now I was an experienced and persistent ghost hunter. Sensing that I was not going to back off readily, Mr. Lacombe kindly invited me to see him in his office at the Legislature Building the next day.

My excitement hadn't waned by the time of our appointment. Despite a protest rally going on in front of the building, I arrived fifteen minutes early.

No matter how tenacious a researcher is, at some point that person must admit that if there is no story, well, there is no story. In this case, I was interviewing the man who should have known. Oscar Lacombe suspects that the story of that ghost is the result of one of his own practical jokes.

As head of security, among other roles, the Sergeant-At-Arms supervises the twenty-four-hour-a-day security guards. Lacombe is a former army man. One of the guards he had hired had been with the air force, and, in Lacombe's opinion, was a little too vocal about his allegiance to that branch of the services. Shortly before the new man was to work his first night-shift, Oscar Lacombe alluded to the fact that the building might be haunted. Not surprisingly, the new guard heard frightening noises all night. That's all it took to start the story, and it has persisted for years.

Despite my attempts to find and record all the ghost stories in Alberta, some have probably been missed. If you have heard a ghost story that hasn't been included in this book, please let me know. There is always the possibility of volume two.

Edmonton Ghost Stories

1: McKay Museum's
Lively Spirits

Do you ever feel haunted by your job? Ron Hlady can certainly sympathize. He's the Building Preservation Technician at McKay Avenue School, which now serves as the Edmonton Public Schools Museum and Archives.

In the early 1980s, the once-grand old school closed its doors to students. Shortly after that, restoration got underway. The site was an obvious one to become an historical treasure house. The first free public school in the Alberta District of the Northwest Territories was located there. Unbelievably, that clapboard structure has survived despite having served numerous functions since its construction in 1881. The building is back in its original condition and location, although now dwarfed by the museum and Edmonton's inevitable growth.

In 1904, McKay Avenue School replaced that original school house and the imposing red brick structure began to earn its own place in the political and educational history of Alberta.

The first and second sittings of the Alberta Legislature were held in the third-floor assembly hall. Youngsters destined to make an impression on the world practised their sums and pored over their readers in the classrooms. Hollywood star Leslie Nielsen, Supreme Court Justice Ronald Martland, the National Hockey League's Clarence Campbell, author Lotta Dempsey and internationally acclaimed air force and bush pilot "Wop" May were all students at McKay.

2

Given this colourful history, a few quirky stories surrounding the building might be expected. The incidents Ron has documented over the years, however, go well beyond quirky.

"The restoration seems to have caused a lot more activity than anyone could have predicted. There's definitely something going on in the building. Some mornings it looks like there's been a party."

That comment was made by a former co-worker of Ron's, who has since sought more mundane employment. It was he who was working with Ron to set up a room for an early morning audio-visual presentation. They spent the last part of their day lining up chairs in neat rows, lowering window blinds and, as a precaution, even stapling them to the sills.

As usual, Ron was the last to leave at night and the first to get to work in the morning. What he found that next morning would have sent a lesser man to the unemployment office. Chairs were knocked over and strewn around the room. Despite the staples, some blinds were up and others were right off the windows.

"We really had to rush in order to redo the room in time for the meeting," explained the unflappable Hlady.

On other occasions, boilers have been turned on or off, doors that were left locked were found unlocked, pictures have been removed from the walls, and the school's security system has registered a rash of false readings. No wonder the other employees aren't keen on staying alone in the old building!

These incidents, coupled with occasional strange tales from visiting alumni, prompted Ron to bring a Ouija board to work. Through the board, "Peter" was quick to identify himself. He maintains there are half a dozen spirits floating around the school. This didn't surprise Ron. The number and variety of occurrences had led him to assume he was dealing with more than one presence. Despite this, Peter's been the only one to communicate with Ron.

What Peter lacks in visibility, he certainly makes up for in personality.

The photos on the bulletin board of the former McKay Avenue School have been found scattered about the room.

He's "told" Ron quite a bit about himself. He was a labourer during construction of the 1912 four-classroom addition to McKay Avenue School. He claims to have been married and the father of three daughters, one of whom is still alive and resides in California.

Peter reports that he was killed in a fall from the roof, and apparently his spirit has roamed the building ever since. He has steadfastly refused to reveal his last name. As labourers in 1912 would have little need to read or write, Peter might well have been illiterate and therefore unable to spell his name to Ron on the Ouija board.

A pair of young psychics, operating a business called Second Sight, were called in. They confirmed there were a number of spirits residing in the building, but disappointingly, Peter did not identify himself to either of them.

The psychics' visit was far from wasted though. While standing in the school hall, the woman reported in an astonished voice, "Children are

The original school was built in 1881 and it opened in 1882.

running up and down the side of the building. How can that be?"

The ever-pragmatic Hlady pointed to the fire-escape stairs on the exterior of the school. They would have been used frequently during routine fire drills.

When another "feeling" stumped the young lady – "My jaw hurts in this room," was her comment at one point during the tour – Ron again came up with an explanation. The room she was in used to be the school's medical room where visiting dentists examined and tended to students' dental problems.

The most dramatic moment of the tour came when everyone involved realized that file-cabinet drawers that were closed upon entering the room were now open. The room this occurred in is on the second floor in the southwest corner of the building.

On the third floor, the psychic was again drawn to the southwest cor-

The 1904 school became a museum, but the presences of a man killed from falling from the roof and of children on the fire escape have lingered.

ner. This time, though, she was embarrassed to find herself in a recently renovated men's washroom! Could this possibly be the area Peter fell from? Likely, no one will ever know, but that corner does overlook the 1881 school house.

The small building was used as a storage shed for tools during the time Peter was working on the addition to the newer school. He would have been in and out of the old wooden building frequently.

Ron is also required to be out at the one-room school house often. The man reports that sometimes when he goes out there, "a wicked shiver" will run through his body. That nostalgic little structure originally opened on January 3, 1882. Peter claims to have died on January 3, 1912. Ron Hlady was born on January 3, 1951. Quite a coincidence.

This story appeared in the September/October 1991 edition of *Teaching Today*. It is re-told here with the permission of that magazine's editorial director, Betty Ann Coderre.

2: Felicia Graham, Where Are You?

Junior high schools can be frightening places. Edmonton's Westmount Junior High School has an extra reason. Her name is Felicia Graham, and the strikingly beautiful school marm has roamed the third-floor halls of the stately old building for nearly seventy-five years.

After obtaining a Master of Arts degree from University College at the University of Toronto, thirty-three-year-old Felicia left her parents' home and came west in 1918. She was assigned to teach English within what was then a radically new educational concept: a junior high school.

By the end of September, Miss Graham was desperately unhappy. This was not an assignment she could ever enjoy, and a transfer to the more traditional Strathcona High School was arranged. Just days before the relocation was to take place, all of Edmonton's public schools were closed. A fatal flu epidemic swept through the province, leaving few families completely intact.

While the outbreak ran its course, three Edmonton schools became makeshift hospitals, and women teachers were recruited as nurses. When the medical crisis was over, teachers and students were called back to classes. Felicia Graham didn't report for duty at either Westmount or Strathcona. In fact, Felicia Graham was never seen again.

The young woman's parents were frantic. They offered an extremely generous reward for information leading to their daughter's whereabouts.

A teacher (in one form or another) may have been roaming the halls of Westmount Junior High School for nearly 75 years.

They were convinced that their offer of $500 cash would procure promising results. Much to their disappointment, they kept the funds. No one has ever been able to say for sure what happened to the well-educated beauty from the east.

Speculation, of course was and is rampant. Was Felicia Graham also a victim of the flu epidemic? Was she unhappy enough with her teaching assignment that she just left the city without notifying anyone? Perhaps she was a victim of women's age-old dilemma: an unwanted, inconvenient and extremely embarrassing pregnancy. That theory might also explain her continuing presence in the halls of Westmount Junior High School. Could the unborn child's father have been a colleague of Felicia's and whose classroom was near the hallway her troubled spirit continues to roam?

3: Strange Events in Clareview Condominium

Albert (a pseudonym) worked with Ron Hlady at the McKay Avenue School (see Chapter 1) and was witness to the results of some "ghostly parties." Considering the following tale, it is little wonder he asked to be transferred to another school.

In 1983, Albert, a caretaker with an Edmonton school board, moved his wife and two sons into a newly built, condominium townhouse project at the eastern edge of Edmonton. Albert and his wife, Sharon, were a friendly, outgoing young couple who had no trouble making friends with their new neighbours. Summer evenings, after the children were safely tucked into bed, it was routine for four or five couples to sit outside in the complex's courtyard enjoying the pleasant weather and one another's company.

All in all, the move to the new area seemed to have been a good one for Albert and his family. Even the location of the complex was special to the couple. The land on which this housing project had been built was once a farm owned by a distant relative of Sharon's. It gave them a feeling of family continuity.

Sadly, the idyllic atmosphere was not destined to last. The first person to realize the family was not alone in the townhouse was a visitor, Sharon's mother. She and Albert's thirteen-year-old son, Mick, were alone in the house. The boy was asleep in his bedroom. A blanket that had been on his bed unexpectedly showed up in the room his grandmother was using.

The incident left the family shaken, but the story would likely have been forgotten if it hadn't been the first in a series of increasingly bizarre occurrences.

"I drove home from work one day and saw our living room drapes flying, opening and closing," the man recalled.

Did it ever occur to him that an intruder may have been in his home, and that going in might be dangerous?

"No," he replied. "I'd felt for a long time that there was some sort of a spirit in the place. I was sure that was what was causing the drapes to move. As soon as I walked in, everything settled down. There was no one in the house at all."

They assumed the ghost had been attracted to their particular unit because Sharon was a descendant of the original farmer. For that reason, in addition to the understandable embarrassment factor, the family said nothing to any neighbours about the extraordinary happenings — nothing, that is, until one fine summer evening. As often happened, a group of young parents had assembled with their lawn chairs in the central courtyard, chatting and drinking coffee. The discovery of a small object lying near where the group had congregated changed not only that meeting but all those which followed. The object? An egg. A common chicken's egg. Nothing unusual, except that Clareview, the subdivision where they lived, was well within the boundary of the city, and this was a farm egg, complete with brown shell. Stranger still, it had not been there when the group assembled, nor had anyone put it there. This brown egg merely appeared from out of nowhere, or nowhere in the present anyway.

Not surprisingly, the egg caused quite a stir in the crowd. Conversations which had ranged from car engines to laundry-detergent prices shifted suddenly to the unexplained happenings that many of the residents had experienced since moving into the complex. Electrical appliances would inexplicably cease to function. No reason for the malfunction could ever be found. In a few days the incapacitated machine would be working as though nothing had ever been wrong with it. Televisions tuned to one channel would suddenly be broadcasting another station's programming. By comparing notes, these townhouse dwellers reached the conclusion that a spirit roamed through the development.

Despite the ghost's general activity within the complex, Sharon and Albert's unit apparently was its favourite "haunt." Was it because the ghost was an ancestor of Sharon's? No, according to the clairvoyant who Albert called in.

The reason for the ghost's special interest in their home was son Mick's age. He had just entered puberty. This tumultuous period is reportedly very attractive to those stranded between here and beyond. As the spirit's activity centred around Mick, that assumption would have been safe for anyone to make.

A particularly frightening occurrence involved the teen-aged Mick and is, unfortunately, poorly documented. One night, as the family slept, Sharon awoke to sounds in Mick's bedroom. Automatically, performing an age-old motherly custom, the sleepy woman made her way to her son's bedside. Instead of settling a child frightened by a nightmare or uncomfortable from a stomach ache, Sharon arrived to find her son there in body only.

"The ghost was speaking through my son," Albert explained. "My wife tried to wake me but couldn't. This is very strange because I'm not a heavy sleeper. Even our younger son wouldn't wake up. It was like we were in some kind of a trance."

The terrified woman was left to deal with her temporarily possessed son. The deep trance-like sleep her husband and other son were in lasted as long as the possession, which ended as suddenly as it began. To this day, Mick has no recollection of his body's strange experience.

He is well aware, though, that during that period it was extremely difficult for him to keep track of his belongings. Things that would be of little interest or value to anyone else would disappear frequently from his room. Then, just as mysteriously, they would reappear in a few days. Pieces of jewellery and money were favourite objects for the spirit to "borrow." Although it was annoying, Mick soon learned not to worry about something like a missing pen knife. From experience, he knew it would be back where he'd left it within a few days.

A family with lesser determination would likely have moved to the opposite end of the city. Albert, Sharon, Mick and younger son, Jonathan, however, decided to tackle the haunting head on. They called in a psychic.

He talked to the ghost. He told the restless spirit the family didn't mind the extraordinary presence as long as there were no further threats to anyone's well being. Apparently the invisible visitor agreed because his presence never again frightened anyone. This is not to say the ghost became an ideal roommate. Far from it. If you've heard the expression "the games people play," well, they're nothing compared to the games the Clareview ghost decided to play.

"My wife's purse disappeared once. We hunted high and low for the thing for several hours. We were the only ones home and neither of us had been outside the house yet that day. After nearly four hours of searching, we accepted its loss and began phoning credit card companies to advise them that our cards may have been stolen. No sooner did we do that than the purse turned up smack in the middle of our bed. Each of us had scoured the entire room several times. If the purse had been there, we would have seen it."

Albert and his family moved from the Clareview townhouse development in 1988, after sharing their lives for five years with exceptionally friendly neighbours and a nuisance of a ghost. The former resident drove past the old place not too long ago. He was surprised to see a junior high school being built directly across the street from the complex. If the ghost had been especially attracted to their unit because of their son's age, one hesitates to think what hijinks might occur now. The school will ensure a constant supply of several hundred children in and around the age of puberty.

4: Former Fire Halls' Spirits

The Edmonton Ambulance Authority has taken over several city fire halls. The arrangement was seen as a sensible one that would substantially reduce costs when the fire department relocated to larger premises. Unfortunately, not all the staff went along for the move. As a result, two Edmonton ambulance stations are haunted.

Details of the hauntings vary but acceptance of the tales is amazingly wide spread. As a student paramedic, Deborah Trumbley was assigned to serve a night shift at Number Five Station in Edmonton's east end. As she was drifting off to sleep, she heard footsteps echoing in the garage area and ambulance doors being slammed.

The next morning she mentioned this to the people she was working with. They were only surprised that she hadn't heard about the resident ghost through the grapevine. Scuttlebutt is divided on how the man died. The mundane version reports the firefighter passed away in his sleep during a night shift. A rather more exciting version says that he fell to his death from the back of a fire truck while responding to a call.

What is certain is that the man's spirit hasn't left the building since. His activities are limited to patrolling the vehicle bays. Perhaps, like the Ghost of Flight 401, the man is determined to keep those who've come after safe from harm.

No one has ever reported seeing the apparition, and the only prank he's ever been credited with was to ring all the station's telephones when all lines were free. The person who bore the brunt of this antic was Sue Evans, an administrative employee of the Ambulance Authority. She had gone to the station specifically to check the phone lines. It would seem that neither the man's spirit, nor his sense of humour died with him.

The ghost of Ambulance Station Five is a loafer compared with the spirit that lives in Number Four. He, too, is a former firefighter, and, although this building also now belongs to Edmonton's ambulance service, the tales of hauntings go back to when it was a fire hall.

The man with the most stories to tell in connection with Station Four is still a firefighter with the Edmonton Fire Department. He agreed to be interviewed only on the promise of anonymity – and so the pseudonym Joe.

During a night shift, Joe was assigned to the watch box, an area near the front of the building. One man per shift is designated to sleep there and he is responsible for the overnight security of the fire hall.

Joe was sleeping when he heard the huge garage doors go up. He woke in a near panic – had he somehow slept through an alarm? No, the building was completely dark and quiet, but the doors stood open. Not knowing what else to do, Joe closed the doors, checked the rest of the station thoroughly, and went back to bed.

The next day he told his captain about the experience because he felt not to do so would be neglectful of his duties. Joe did ask his superior, though, to keep it confidential: if his co-workers heard about the incident, Joe knew he would be in for an unbearable amount of teasing.

The next incident also occurred when Joe was in the watch box. This time something awakened him from a sound sleep. He felt tremendously uncomfortable and was convinced that something unusual had awakened him.

He got up immediately and hurried to the dorm. All the men were in their beds, sleeping soundly. Just as he was about to leave the room, a door at the far end of the room swung open and then closed again. Joe felt chilled to the bone.

Old fire hall #4 was renovated, but stories of its former residents linger.

Again he told his boss and again asked that the information go no further. The captain told Joe of a former firefighter who had died in the hall. Jake Smith was reputed to be a hard-living and well-respected member of the Edmonton Fire Department. Could this be who was disturbing Joe's sleep? Quite likely, Jake seemed to be the probable spirit.

The only other time Jake made himself known to Joe was a summer afternoon. All the men were outside when Joe went back into the station. There, he clearly heard a man's voice in an adjacent hallway and felt the now-familiar feeling of extreme discomfort; no one else was inside the building.

Not long after that, the fire department moved to new quarters, and work was done on the station to make it suitable for its new purpose, an ambulance station.

During the renovations, Joe had occasion to drop into the hall. He chatted briefly with one of the workers about the progress being made.

"I'm working as quickly as I can," the man told Joe. "The sooner I'm out of here, the better I'll like it. This place really gives me the creeps."

Joe knew exactly what the man meant.

This story originally appeared in the November 1990 edition of *Canadian Emergency News*. It is retold here with the permission of its editor, Kevin Blades.

5: *Lobotomized Labourer Lives On In Radio*

Radio station CKUA is located in a building on Edmonton's main downtown thoroughfare, Jasper Avenue. To call the Alberta Block nondescript would be a compliment. Few would call it anything short of downright ugly. The only interesting architectural feature is that it is not, in fact, just one building but two, constructed one behind the other and joined together as an afterthought. Inside the building it is easy to tell by the odd shape of the corridors that there have been "renovations."

What the structure lacks in visual charm it makes up for in interesting history. The block dates back to the early days of this century. It started out as a flophouse. Although there have been many structural changes since those early days, remnants of the original use remain. For instance, some rooms still contain stove plugs and kitchen cupboards. The Alberta Block also probably boasts a greater number of unused vaults per square foot than any other building in the province.

Technician Larry King explained that because the premises were used by Alberta Safety Services during the Second World War, disaster evacuation plans were stored in vaults on the site. The Alberta Treasury Branch also had offices in the building, and they, of course, also required vaults. None has ever been removed.

CKUA is not a mainstream commercial radio station. It originated as the University of Alberta's station, continued as an educational service, and now broadcasts programs that focus on the arts. Each program has its own characteristics and following.

As an employer, the station must be exceptionally good. Even in today's mobile job market, employees tend to stay on. Twenty years seniority is not unusual for the staff there. One and possibly two former employees have stayed at their place of employment even after death.

Credit for the building's haunted status most commonly goes to Sam, a former janitor. Even in life he was a mysterious character. Sam started with the station in the mid-1950s and remained employed there until his death in the 1970s. Bill Coull, a long-time radio station employee and accomplished media person, remembers Sam clearly.

"He'd had quite the career in the east, I understand. It was said that he'd been a member of the "Stern Gang" during the 1940s and that he had connections in the Middle East. He was also supposed to have a wife and lots of property in Toronto."

Why would such a man be working as a janitor then? It seems Sam's lifestyle caught up with him when he threatened the life of then-Premier Ernest Manning. Perhaps because of his checkered past, the verbal attack was taken seriously. Seen as a menace to public safety, Sam was lobotomized. It was this docile shell of a human who swept the floors at CKUA.

Sam's love of opera did not disappear with his brain's frontal lobe. He would spend a great deal of time in the station's enormous record library poring over recordings of operas and could frequently be heard singing arias.

"He was a strange person," explained Coull. "He was very polite and quiet. I never saw him without a cigar or pipe in his mouth. He was a big guy, six foot four; he had the strange blank look of a dullard; he never laughed and when he did speak it was with a slight accent."

Most of the staff at CKUA have become aware of Sam's ghostly presence at one time or another. Some have heard his clear tenor voice on the other side of the library stacks when they were in that area. Others have experienced the distinct impression that someone was in a room with them when, as far as they could tell, they were actually by themselves.

Bill has actually seen what may well be Sam's apparition.

"It was about 1:00 a.m., and I felt a presence. The lighting was dim, but when I looked up I saw the reflection of a face on the control-room glass. I could only clearly make out the eyes and a cigar."

Larry King has been made very aware of the building's ghost. Never having seen the spirit, he does wonder if it is Sam who is responsible for the haunting.

"I've certainly experienced a ghost's presence, but I've always wondered if it was a former fellow technician. The man was from the same town I was. He trained at the Southern Alberta Institute of Technology just a few years before I did, and then he came here to work just ahead of me. Shortly after that, he died of leukemia. He was somewhat of a mentor to me, and as this spirit is an extremely helpful one I thought at one time that it might have been him."

Like all CKUA's employees, Larry would just as soon never go to the basement of the building. Unfortunately, most do have need to go there now and again. Also, like most of his colleagues Larry frequently experiences the sensation that he is not alone. This feeling came frequently when he worked the graveyard shift.

"Quite often I'd feel there was someone watching me," he acknowledged.

One night, when a tape machine broke down, Larry had to carry it to the floor below for repairs. The machine was heavy and awkward, and Larry needed both of his hands to manage the load. To add to his burden, the technician had the familiar impression that he was being watched.

"It gave me a prickly sensation, the shivers," he remembered.

When Larry got to the bottom of the flight of stairs, he puzzled a moment over how to open the "crash" hardware on the door. With neither hand free, his options were limited. He turned around to give the bar a firm hip check. Just as he did, the door flew open and the overloaded technician nearly fell into the hallway with the tape machine on top of him.

Larry is convinced the spirit was not trying to cause an accident but merely attempting to be helpful. Even so, it's easy to appreciate why the man is grateful he no longer has to work the graveyard shift.

In the meantime, the ghost's presence continues to be felt on occasion by most CKUA employees.

6: Someone's in the Kitchen with Dinah

In the late 1970s, the Norwood area of Edmonton was a delightful residential community of older homes. The tree-lined streets provided a congenial alternative to the barren suburbs that had flourished as a result of the recent oil boom. Unfortunately, the years have not been kind to the area. Now it is rundown and seedy, an area for those with ghosts of their own making haunting their very existence.

It was not today's Norwood, though, that Dinah chose. And so, when she bought the two-storey house on a corner lot she looked forward to calling the place home for years to come. This sort of stability of residence was especially important to the woman at that time because after working for a number of years as a horticulturist, Dinah began making a career change. She was returning to the University of Alberta as a graduate student and very much looking forward to the positive effects these changes would have on her life.

"When I moved in to the house, I was living with a man. The relationship was pretty well over by that time. It wasn't good at all any more," Dinah explained.

The short time the two lived together in the 1918 house was not a pleasant time for either of them.

"We would both wake up suddenly in the middle of the night and neither of us would know why. This went on for weeks and it became very draining," she said.

Shortly after, the two parted company and Dinah continued to live in the house, alone.

"There was definitely a presence in the house. The ghost, or spirit, or whatever it was, restricted itself to the kitchen. It was a real nuisance, though. Things would go missing from the kitchen and then turn up again a day or so later exactly where they should have been. One morning I was getting ready to leave for a very important day at school. Some papers I needed were nowhere to be found. I spoke to the ghost. I told it I was getting thoroughly fed up with its tricks and that I needed the papers it had taken."

Dinah advised the mysterious presence that she was going out for a short walk and when she returned she expected those papers would be put back where they had been.

"I did as I'd said I would, and sure enough when I came back the papers were on the counter where I'd left them the night before."

Whoever was in the kitchen with Dinah must have been a free spirit: it didn't adapt well to living under the control of this vibrant and energetic woman's commands. Just a few weeks after the man she'd been living with left, so did the ghost, and Dinah was finally able to gain complete "living alone" status. Happily, neither the ghost nor the companion have ever entered the Norwood home since.

7: Ghostly Bookworm?

Edmonton is a city of shopping malls. It is home not only to the gigantic West Edmonton Mall but also to dozens of cookie-cutter-same retail groupings. The shops along Whyte Avenue in old Strathcona area are a pleasant diversion from this routine sameness.

In 1986, a former school teacher added to the ambience of the neighbourhood and realized a lifelong dream at the same time. Donna Tremblay (a pseudonym) opened Gryphon Books. The buildings along the popular strip are old by Edmonton standards. Some date back to the 1800s, many to the early 1900s. It was such a building that housed the newly opened bookstore. The owner was aware that the shop had, at various times, been a millinery store, a clothing store and, once, even a shooting gallery.

As the bookstore was the fruition of many years of thought and planning, Donna expected few surprises. The first several months of operation were, in fact, completely uneventful at Gryphon Books. Then, just as the new endeavour began to feel comfortable, strange things began to happen. One morning, when she unlocked the store, Donna found books lying on the floor.

"There were books piled in stacks at various places around the store," the proprietor explained.

She was more than a little surprised, but because "the show had to go on" and the store had to open, Donna quickly filed the volumes back where they had been and opened the store for another day of business.

That particular occurrence set a precedent for Gryphon Books and, over time, a pattern developed. Every morning there were books out of place. Whoever or whatever was doing the re-arranging clearly had certain places in the store that he, she or it preferred.

"Most often there were books stacked near the cash register or by the staircase leading to the basement," Donna explained and then added that she became used to these occurrences and merely scheduled sufficient time for tidying up before opening. The fact that an unseen, unfelt, and unheard presence seemed to want to have a hand in running her business did not really bother the proprietor. The easy-going and confident lady merely accepted the inconvenience and worked around it.

Several months later, concerned about both health and safety, the store owner hung "No Smoking" signs around the store. The next morning they were on the floor. Presuming they'd only fallen, Donna re-hung them and opened the store for the day. All went well for two days. Then the signs were not found merely lying on the floor: one "No Smoking" sign was found nearly twelve feet from its original place, another was hidden behind some books on another shelf, and the third was found by the front door. The signs had clearly offended the ghost of Gryphon Books.

By trial and error, Donna found that if she hung only one sign and only in a particular spot by the front of the store, it would remain in place. The unseen bookworm was not, however, as easily satisfied where the merchandise was concerned. During the entire time Donna Tremblay owned the store, books were sorted through and re-stacked each and every night. Every morning the owner would re-shelf the stacks and then open the store for business.

There never seemed to be any malevolence motivating the mischievous spirit, but he or she certainly was long suffering. Like the shoemaker's elves, the spirit worked on, unseen every night Donna Tremblay owned the business.

8: The Wing's
Voices

The staff of some of Alberta's haunted places take great pleasure in acknowledging that fact in their particular venues. They enjoy the status a resident ghost gives them, including a bit of extra public exposure, free advertising, and possibly additional customers. Other buildings are widely accepted as being haunted, but management's "official" stance is that this is not so. As is often the case, the denial seems to reflect their concern about their public image.

The following tale, about a well-known Edmonton landmark, falls in the latter category. Once a public building, this particular haunted place was purchased several years ago by an adjacent business. Their official opinion is that they've never heard or seen anything unusual about the place and do not wish to discuss the issue further.

The strange tales began to surface shortly after the building was bought by private industry. It is an enormous shell of a building and its private function was to be very different from its public one. The purchase itself was a risky one because of the tremendous amount of money required to make the place over for its new purpose.

Fortunately for this anthology, a personable young employee felt the building's story was too good to be ignored. With the promise of anonymity for himself and non-identifying references to his employer, he spoke comfortably and at length. His suggestion of referring to the building by its standard nickname, The Wing, has been adhered to.

As with many witnesses to strange occurrences, this young man, whom we'll call Ken, began his conversation by making excuses for his experiences.

"It's a big old barn of a building," he began. "That's probably part of what makes it so spooky. That and buying it was such a great financial risk for my employer. It was definitely a transition period for the company. Everything seemed to have a feeling of uncertainty during those first weeks."

Ken's voice clearly reflected the discomfort he had felt at the time. Launching the necessary massive renovations did absolutely nothing to ease the discomfort everyone agreed they felt in the enormous and nearly empty building.

"Nearly" is the pivotal word in the last sentence. Although there weren't a great number of objects left behind, one in particular was quite outstanding: a fighter plane.

"It was an actual fighter, right there in the building. It had to be dismantled in order to be removed. The job took about two dozen people," Ken explained. "Moving the plane out seemed to start a lot of bizarre tales from our staff. Lots of times they'd tell me that they could hear people talking when they were cleaning up after banquets. The voices were always off in the distance, where none of our staff were. I never paid much attention to the stories; I'd never had the experience myself. I did know that I was never very happy about being in that building alone but I could never put my finger on exactly why I felt that way."

One night this hardworking young man was given a very concrete reason.

"It was late and I was giving the place a last check before locking up for the night. Everyone else had left. As I entered the building, I heard a piano being played. The music was clear and beautiful. It was most definitely coming from inside the building."

Despite the man's love of music, he turned and fled from the sounds. Stories continue to crop up now and again. The man listens with more interest now.

"It doesn't surprise me any more when I hear reports of unexplainable experiences in or around The Wing."

Very recently a dance group was using the place to rehearse. One of the young women approached Ken before she boarded the bus for their next destination.

"You know," the shaken dancer began, "as I was leaving the building the thought came to me that I'd forgotten something."

Ken politely indicated that such an experience could happen to anyone, and he wondered what she could possibly have left behind that could have distressed her so much that her voice was shaking.

"But this wasn't like that," she protested. "You see, it wasn't my thought."

9: Cafe Painter
Has Company

Walter Embo introduced himself to me in a most unusual way. After listening to radio-station CKUA's interview about my search for local ghost stories, Walter mailed me a short note describing himself as "Peter's neighbour" (see Chapter 1). Indeed, the return address on the envelope was just around the corner from the Edmonton Public Schools' Museum and Archives.

While listening to the broadcast, Walter realized he had some information that might be useful. I called him the same day I received his note and suggested we meet at Rigoletto's, a downtown cafe.

After brief pleasantries, Walter looked around the dimly lit cafe a bit uncomfortably. I wondered if I should have chosen a different spot. The man seemed distinctly ill at ease. This seemed such a contradiction to the witty note he'd gone to the trouble of writing to me. I hoped that Walter had not changed his mind about telling me of his experience. Disappointingly, this had happened a couple of times in my hunt for stories. Thankfully, that was not the case this time. It was, however, discomfort that I detected.

"It's strange that you picked this spot," he said quietly. "In 1985, this restaurant changed hands. The new owner was an acquaintance of mine and I was looking for extra work, so

I took on the job of painting the restaurant for him. I'd forgotten, until you mentioned Rigoletto's as a meeting spot, that I'd had an experience here that I've never been able to explain."

Walter worked at the painting contract alone in the evenings. Occasionally, to get the job finished on schedule, he was still there, brush in hand, well into the wee hours of the morning. Right from the first day, Walter felt a presence in the restaurant with him. As painting walls and ceilings does not require very much intellectual power, he was free to concentrate on the strange feeling. The more Walter focused on it, the more convinced he became that he was not alone.

"I don't know what it was, but I know it was there. I suppose you could call it a ghost but I don't really know what a ghost is, so I hesitate to call it anything. I do know for sure, though, that there was something there with me those evenings. It gave me a very positive feeling. I came to enjoy the company and even began to talk to whatever was out there."

The spirit must have enjoyed either the recognition or Walter or both because it began to manifest itself physically. When he spoke to it, Walter would see little sparks of light darting about the room and feel gentle puffs of air gusting.

"Whatever it was never spoke back to me, yet I felt as though there had been dialogue. The energy was very childlike, not totally developed, and yet it felt very informed." Walter paused and then added, "It's been years since I've thought of that experience and if you hadn't suggested Rigoletto's as a meeting place I probably never would have again. When I contacted you, it was to tell you of a completely different experience I had while living in a house in downtown Edmonton."

10: Uninvited Guests

Appearing relieved to have the first story told and off his mind, Walter settled in to his café au lait and the tale he'd originally intended to share with me.

The Boyle Street area of Edmonton has been skid row for dozens of years. Few people deliberately choose to live there; most live there as a consequence of choices they made years ago. In January 1982 there were at least four exceptions to that generality. Walter Embo was one of them.

Boyle Street may be the worst of Edmonton's slums, but it is also undeniably convenient to downtown. A friend of Walter's had moved to the area just for that reason. When a neighbouring house became vacant, he suggested Walter would also enjoy being within walking distance of the city core and a deal was struck.

The slums of any city are old and rickety; they reflect the human turmoil they've housed. Neatly tailored lots with fences and clean property lines found in the affluent suburbs don't exist around the homes of Walter and his friends.

There were four houses on two lots: two large ones facing onto the street, each with a smaller one in its backyard. It was while living in one of the small ones that Walter had an unpleasant, unexplained and unforgettable encounter.

"On January 2, 1982, I came home from work extremely tired. As soon as I went into the house, I felt someone was there. I heard noises upstairs and so I went up to check. There was nothing there, but as soon as I'd gotten upstairs I heard noises downstairs."

Being tired and feeling grateful to at last be at home, Walter was only mildly upset by the unexplained noises.

Edmonton's harsh, dreary winters are well documented, but most residents have devised favourite ways of coping. Many like to remind themselves that spring's warmth and beauty will eventually return. Walter's way of doing that was to force plant bulbs on his kitchen window. The protective cones over these bulbs were the only things he could see that had moved as a result of the noises he'd heard.

Puzzled, the man stared at the pots on his windowsill. As he did, two of the paper cones lifted off the bulbs and came to rest on their sides a few inches away. With increasing concern, Walter replaced the cones and went about trying to make himself as comfortable as he could be.

"I felt little movements everywhere and I was so cold. No matter what I did I couldn't get that house to warm up. I even had the kitchen stove turned on but still I couldn't get warm."

Thinking his exhaustion was causing at least some of the trouble, Walter headed for bed. He felt extremely uncomfortable and couldn't sleep. Soon he got back up and wandered aimlessly through the house. As Walter stood staring out the window of his back door, he was delighted to see his friend in the larger house on the same property doing the same thing.

"The man was in his pyjamas. He had a housecoat on but it was not done up. As soon as I waved to him, he did up the belt and then waved back. I knew there was no way I was going to be able to sleep for awhile and, as my friend was also awake, I decided to go and visit him. We chatted in his kitchen and after a few minutes he asked me if I didn't have to be going. I thought this was a strange comment and I asked why he thought I should leave."

"Why? Because you have guests, don't you? I saw someone standing behind you when you were at the door waving to me. I didn't have my glasses on so I couldn't make out whether it was a man or a woman, but there was definitely someone there. That's why I did my housecoat up."

Walter was shaken by his friend's statements and attempted to explain what had just happened to him. He asked his neighbour to watch while he returned across the back yard to the little house that he used to enjoy calling home. As any good friend and neighbour would, this man agreed and he phoned Walter as soon as he saw him go through the door.

"Someone went into the house right after you," the man said.

For three days Walter Embo went almost entirely without sleep. "I worked late trying to get tired enough to sleep and also to avoid coming home."

The pain he'd experienced ten years before was clearly visible on his face as he was relating this story.

"After about ten days, the uncomfortable intensity began to lift. A few days later, it was gone entirely," he said.

Shortly after that, one of the larger of the two houses at the front of the properties came vacant and Walter moved in. As a friend had done for him a few months before, Walter informed another friend that the little house was available. His friend lived there for over three years and if he ever had any strange experiences he never told Walter.

11: The Chinese Ghost of 115 Street

"Ask Madeline Smithers about the Chinese ghost of 115 Street," Edmonton writer and historian Tony Cashman recommended.

The lady was pleasant but admitted, "He's not really my ghost. He belongs to my neighbour. It's a wonderful story. I'll give you the man's name and phone number."

After leaving several messages for the neighbour that were not returned, it became obvious the man did not wish to discuss his occasional visitor. Fortunately, Madeline (a pseudonym) knew at least the framework of the story.

The Oliver area of Edmonton was, at one time, home to some of the city's most affluent families. Many had servants, and an especially loyal Chinese house-boy is still seen every now and again. Dressed in the traditional black silk "pyjamas", the long-deceased immigrant continues to circulate among guests when the older families who remain in the area entertain in their gardens.

The helpful spirit must have worked for a neighbourhood family around the turn of the century. Since then, the area has changed dramatically. Highrise apartment buildings have, to a large degree, replaced the stately old homes. There is no way of telling whether the residence the ghost was affiliated with during his lifetime still exists or not. It is obvious, though, that serving at garden parties was a major component of the man's duty roster.

Owners of the few single family homes that remain in the coveted location are not surprised when one of their guests comments on the unusual waiter. Did the hosts hire the man specifically for the occasion? Well, no, in fact they did not.

His turn-of-the-century employer may not even have been located in the Oliver area. The loyal servant's spirit may have drifted from his own area when urban renewal ended the ambience he loved. The 115 Street locale may well have attracted his soul because garden parties are still occasionally given there.

What is known about the house-boy is that he only appears during outdoor galas. He mingles with the crowd, always seeming to be busy and never approaching any particular guest. His distinctive attire isn't the only way to recognize the deceased immigrant. He gives another, equally unmistakable clue as to his identity. The ghost of 115 Street is not quite solid. Most guests don't notice at first, but the Chinese house-boy dressed in traditional garb is slightly see-through.

As the garden parties in the Oliver area disappear, will the ghostly servant vanish completely?

Equally puzzling is the unwillingness of Madeline Smithers's neighbour to discuss the spirit. A presence as widely accepted as this one would be difficult for anyone to dismiss completely. Perhaps the man enjoys his association with the phantom and does not want to share him.

12: The House
on the Hill

Madeline Smithers (a pseudonym) is one of those rare women whose youthful beauty has not faded with the years. It has only mellowed and matured. Today, in her seventies, Madeline's still-exquisite face, radiates vibrance and enthusiasm. Life has not tarnished this lady in any way.

When she was a child, Madeline's parents lived in Drumheller. Wanting a proper education for their daughter, they sent the child to a convent school in Red Deer. During these years, report cards on each student's progress went home, by mail, to the children's parents; the students were left blissfully unaware of their academic improvement or lack of it.

Madeline's world was a happy one, if geographically limited. It consisted of school at the convent and vacation times at home in Alberta's Badlands. As many teenage girls do, the young woman began to experience recurring dreams.

"I would dream I was standing on a river bank looking up at a white house on a hill," she explained. "In the early 1950s when we moved here to Edmonton, I recognized it immediately. This was the house I'd dreamed of over and over again. When I first walked in, I felt the house welcomed me."

It was amazing that her adolescent and subconscious mind had known that she'd live in this house, especially as it is a very unusual one. Most Edmonton residences line the city's streets or avenues. Madeline's home is perched on the river bank, and the only road access to it is via a series of back alleys.

Despite the house's unusual location and Madeline's youthful dreams, the question remains, why would this lively and down-to-earth lady think her home was haunted?

"Because I've seen the ghost," came the straightforward reply. "She's a beautiful young blonde woman. She's played several tricks on me over the years."

One night as Madeline was going up to bed for the night, a paper on the stairs caught her eye.

"It was one of my report cards from the convent in Red Deer. How would it have gotten here?" she asked rhetorically. "I'd never seen it before in my life."

That certainly didn't diminish Madeline's interest in it now. Even after all these years, the lady's inquisitive nature had to be satisfied.

"It was from the year that I was eight. All my marks were 'Very Good' – except the 'C' I got for 'Silence'. But, to this day I have no idea how that card came to be in this house. It just appeared."

Madeline is an accomplished potter. During a time she was taking pottery classes, she came home with a sheaf of papers that had been handed out. The middle few pages were "recipes" for different clays and baking procedures. The next day, when a friend asked to check some information on one of those sheets, Madeline picked the stapled photocopies up from where she'd left them on the dining room table. She was amazed to discover several sheets missing from the stack although the staples showed no signs of having been tampered with. Years went by before Madeline ever saw those sheets again.

"Do you know where they turned up?" she asked. "They were in the top middle drawer of the sideboard in the dining room. That's where I keep my table linens. I'd been in and out of that drawer several times a week, every week since the recipes went missing. They weren't hidden under anything, either; they were lying, one beside the other, on top of what's stored in the drawer. I couldn't have missed them if they'd been there before."

The fact that Madeline lives alone in her scrupulously well-kept home only added to the puzzle.

"She just likes to play games," was the only explanation Madeline could think to offer. "The only other trick she's ever played on me was to take curtain rods that a friend and I had bought and spread them all across the floor."

While she is playing these tricks, Mrs. Smithers's ghost has only made herself visible on one occasion.

"I was alone in the house, reading. I felt someone was there beside me. I looked up and straight into the eyes of a young woman. She didn't frighten me in the least. She was only curious. She was so beautiful. Her face was right next to mine and she was staring at me intently."

Madeline is not the only one to have become aware of the ghostly presence in the house on the hill. A university student stayed there to look after the place while Madeline was away. She was awakened in the middle of the night by a presence in her bedroom.

Although the startled girl could not see the apparition, she felt it touch her face. Understandably frightened, she cut short her "house sitting" assignment, reporting that whatever it was in that room had definitely not wanted her in the house.

If a "standard" explanation for this ghost story is wanted, it might be that a former occupant so loved the house that she's refused to leave it, even in death. Unfortunately, Mrs. Smithers's story refuses to be so neatly pigeon-holed.

"The people we bought this house from were the original owners, a middle-aged man and his elderly mother. No young woman has ever lived here."

Is it possible, then, that somehow the beautiful young apparition was Madeline Smithers herself, perhaps her young spirit somehow arrested in time?

A delightful peal of girlish laughter accompanied the reply. "Oh no, not a chance. I was never that pretty."

13: Dream House Turns to Nightmare

Lana and Mike Rose were ecstatic when they found their dream home, complete with a white picket fence, in the pleasant Westmount area of Edmonton.

"We were newly married and full of vim. The house was just what we were looking for. It was very old-fashioned and needed repairs, but that was a challenge we both looked forward to," Lana recalled.

Some of the features that indicated the home's age were ones they would carefully maintain. Both Lana and Mike considered the hardwood floors and enormous bathtub on legs to be treasures. There were other features in the house, though, that Lana especially would much rather have done without.

"The basement stairs led off the kitchen. They were narrow and steep. There was no light switch to turn on before you went down. You had to go to the bottom of the stairs and then to the middle of the room before you could turn on a light in the basement," Lana remembered. To make matters worse, the furnace was the old octopus-style, with pipes criss-crossing the basement. Their wringer-washer would only fit in one corner, and the furnace pipes blocked most of the light the single bulb in the ceiling provided.

"It got so I'd only do washing during the day, when there was a bit of sunshine coming through the basement window," Lana added.

Even with this precaution, Lana was not comfortable in the basement.

"Every time I was downstairs, I could hear someone walking upstairs. I would run up to see who was there but no one ever was. These weren't heavy steps, but light and slow. I locked the back and front doors and told myself the noises were just in my imagination because I didn't like being down there."

It's easy to sympathize with the young woman's dislike for the cellar area of the house, but compared to the second storey, the basement was cosy. The stairway to the partial second storey also led off the kitchen. Like the one to the basement, it was also narrow and steep. The bedroom at the top of the stairs was tiny, with only room for a single bed and a hutch.

"The bedroom had a board about three feet by three feet, with a frame around it," Lana recalled. "It was the entrance to the attic. We kept this closed with a hook and eye on one side and hinges on the other."

To be more accurate, they tried to keep it closed.

"The hook and eye never stayed closed, which was a puzzle to me." Lana paused and added, "It was like someone kept opening it."

Shortly after Lana and Mike moved into the house, they invited Lana's sister and baby son to stay with them. The arrangement only lasted a fortnight and left everyone's lives changed.

"My nephew was having his nap in the upstairs bedroom. Suddenly he let out a horrible scream. My sister and I both ran up the stairs. The door to the attic was open wide!" The terror the two young women had felt was evident even after all these years. "I phoned my father and he came right over. He searched and found nothing, so he closed the hook and eye again and also jammed a knife into the attic doorway."

Thinking all would be well now with his daughters and grandson, the man left. But, he'd only been gone a few minutes when noises could be heard coming from the empty room above.

"I thought I'd better check it out. I didn't want to go up there because I was so scared, but my dad had gone and I couldn't reach my husband. I went upstairs very cautiously. The knife had been taken out of the attic entranceway and was lying about three feet from where my father had jammed it in. The knife certainly had not just fallen out of the crack and rolled all that distance."

Attempting to salvage what was left of the afternoon, Lana gave her young nephew his favourite toy, the stuffed monkey that he had taken to bed with him before all the commotion.

"He took one look at it and screamed," the child's concerned aunt said. "He never played with that monkey again and any time we tried to take him up to the bedroom he cried. Something had frightened him badly."

Feeling their dream home had turned to a nightmare, the newlyweds and their boarders moved out less than two weeks later. They felt the presence had made its wishes clear. The little family was not welcome in "his" home.

14: Little Girl in White

As we shall see with the next two stories, children and their
bedrooms are often implicated in hauntings.

E nid McCalla is a dedicated young mother. In the mid-
1980s, she and her daughter Candyce were living in a
Millwoods townhouse. The child was three years old and the apple of her
mother's eye.

One night, several hours after Enid had put Candyce to bed, the little
girl uttered a series of piercing shrieks. Racing from her room to the
child's bedside, Enid found the child sitting up in bed, clutching the covers around her, and staring at the end of her bed with eyes as big as saucers.

"Mommy, Mommy, there's a little girl sitting on my bed," the frightened child wailed.

Of course, Enid could clearly see that there was no one else in the
room; she also knew that her daughter had suffered a childhood nightmare. She set about easing the child's distress. Unfortunately, Enid wasn't
able to calm the badly scared youngster, and in order that both of them
would be able to sleep, Enid carried Candyce down the hall and tucked
the child into bed with her.

The next morning the child still had a vivid recollection of her experience through the night. At breakfast she described, in detail, the vision that had so frightened her.

"It was a little girl, Mom. She was wearing a long white nightie and she wouldn't stop staring at me. She scared me," the child explained.

"It was only a bad dream, sweetheart. Mommy checked all around your room and there was no one there. You imagined it," the mother offered comfortingly.

"No, Mommy. It wasn't a bad dream. She really was in my room."

Seeing that pressing the issue was only going to make matters worse, the sensible young Enid changed the subject. Thankfully, it doesn't take much to get a three-year-old's mind off something.

Months later, early one sunny morning, Enid was baking a cake. The kitchen was brightly lit from sun streaming in the adjacent dining room window. In a quiet way, the young mother was enjoying preparing the dessert she intended to serve that evening.

Suddenly, out of the corner of her eye, Enid thought she saw something. Quickly turning her head to catch a better glimpse, Enid realized there was nothing there and went back to mixing the flour. No sooner had she re-started than something moving distracted her again. Because it came from near the ceiling, Enid presumed it was a fly. She looked again. It was not any sort of an insect.

There, sitting suspended in mid-air, was a little girl in a white nightie. The child stared down intently at Enid for a second or two and then disappeared. Badly shaken, Enid dropped the ingredients she'd been working with and leaned against the counter. What was even stranger than the vision was that somehow the child seemed familiar. A few seconds later, Enid's mind cleared sufficiently from the fright to realize where the sense of familiarity came from. This must have been the little girl who'd been sitting on Candyce's bed those many weeks ago.

The little visitor must only have been curious about Enid and Candyce because her presence was never felt again.

15: Poltergeist Prompts People to Pay

In 1987 the Talbot family purchased a small, two-bedroom bungalow in Edmonton's Parkview district. The neighbourhood was an established one. Most of the houses were about thirty-five years old at that time.

Ian Talbot was especially pleased when the deal on the little house was finalized. For some reason he wanted the house desperately and anticipated living there happily for years to come.

Shortly after they moved in, Ian was taking a bath and he heard voices from an adjoining room.

"The house was new to us, and so I just let it go. I really didn't give it much thought," he explained.

When a week later he had the same experience, his curiosity was admittedly peaked. Shortly after that second occurrence, both Ian and his wife shared a bizarre experience.

"We were in bed at night and out of the blue the quilt flew off the bed," he remembered.

At this point they began to search the house carefully for clues. They did not mention anything of the concerns to their daughter whose bedroom was in the basement. Typical of most parents, the Talbots did not want to worry the young woman, especially after she periodically complained of the lights in her bedroom flickering.

The only trace of any former occupant they ever turned up was from some literature about the building's original furnace and water heater. These had apparently been bought many years ago by a "Mr. Wilson."

"From then on my wife and I referred to the ghost as Mr. Wilson. The funny thing was, though, we were both under the impression that the presence was actually a child. It was so playful. Nothing bad ever happened."

Ian concedes, though, that they could have been wrong about the spirit being a child's because the voice they heard was always the same: that of an adult male.

During the four years the family lived in the house, Mr. Wilson rarely let them forget his existence. When guests were leaving one evening, the street lights in front of the Talbot's home inexplicably flickered for a prolonged period. Causing lights to flicker was one of Mr. Wilson's favourite attention-getters.

"We went through a couple of weeks when the clock radio would come on at midnight. It certainly wasn't set for that time. One year we were planning a skiing vacation in Whitefish. When we needed to refer to the brochures we'd collected about the area, they were not where we'd left them. We finally gave up looking and just blamed Mr. Wilson. I suspect we were right because all the brochures turned up again a few days later. They were in a drawer, on top of some socks!"

Ian was still extraordinarily fond of the house and had no intention of moving. He referred to the ghost's pranks as "silly little things." He was a bit alarmed, though, when another daughter, an RCMP constable, came for a visit. She slept in the back bedroom and reported hearing footsteps followed by a door slamming when there was no one else in the house.

If the ghost was actually Mr. Wilson, the man from the past had a fascination with today's electronic appliances.

"He liked to play with our VCR," Ian remembered. "It would come on in the middle of the night; at other times the clock would flash '12:00' – on and off – like it does if the machine has been unplugged. It hadn't been unplugged because there'd been no one home to unplug it and there hadn't been a power failure because all the rest of the clocks were running on time."

An opportunity came up for the family to move to the country. They seized the chance and moved out of their haunted Parkview bungalow in 1991. Oddly, they sold the house for more than the asking price. That was strange enough, but the Talbots had paid more than the asking price when they'd bought it, which made it a double real-estate oddity.

"On moving day as I left the empty house my last words were, 'Goodbye, Mr. Wilson'."

Ian Talbot does not keep in touch with the new owners, but he has no reason to believe that they, too, do not hear voices while they are soaking in the little home's bathtub.

16: Son's Suicide
Haunts House

This story is re-told in its entirety. It's one of those stories where the missing details are as intriguing as those that are known. Also fascinating is people's infinite ability to adapt their lives to bizarre circumstances. Like so many of the tales collected here, this one took place only a few years ago.

Shortly after an Edmonton couple moved into their new home, the husband returned from work and called out a greeting to his wife. He was surprised when she didn't answer him. He'd been expecting she'd be at home before he was.

As he entered the kitchen, the man was shocked to find a large pool of blood near the stove. He checked through the house and, not finding her, called the police and the hospitals. While all this was going on, his wife arrived home, unharmed. She knew nothing of the blood. The kitchen floor had been clean when she left the house hours before.

Shortly after that incident, the couple began to hear sounds and detect movements in the house. They owned dogs. One day when the new owners got home from work, their dogs were uncharacteristically restless. Looking around the house, they found all the chairs in the dining room had been moved. This was the first of what was to become a routine pattern. Every time the couple returned home, they would find their dogs distraught and various pieces of furniture moved.

The couple liked the house and wanted to stay there, but, not surprisingly, they were alarmed by what was happening. They checked into the history of their new home and found that the son of a previous owner had killed himself there. Their attempts to learn more details were fruitless, but that much information was, at least, some explanation. To this day, the couple share their home with their dogs and a furniture-moving ghost.

17: Pixie
Returns

Couples whose children have grown and left home often create strong bonds with their pets. A dog or a cat frequently becomes an important member of their reduced family. This could well be a contributing factor in the following story. Also, when hauntings happen in such couples' homes, they often take place in the bedroom.

In the late 1970s, friends of Marion and Ernie Clarke's gave them a Siamese kitten. The couple's children were grown and living away from home, and so the extra company was welcome. They named the ball of fur "Pixie" and the cat became an important member of their household.

"She was a very intelligent cat," Marion reported. "And she didn't get into mischief like other ones we've had. Her only fault was she liked to sit in cars and sun herself."

Pixie was even willing to override instinct to remain with the Clarkes.

"My husband collected and spawned tropical fish. Pixie loved to go downstairs with him while he was tending to the fish. She was fascinated with all the activity in the different tanks. If she got too close, all Ernie had to do was tell her, 'that's a no-no', and she'd jump back up on her perch."

Pixie's favourite time, though, was bedtime. She would wait for Marion and Ernie to go to bed. Then the comfort-loving cat would jump up on the bed and crawl under the covers to their feet. This was the routine the three Clarkes kept up for years. It was only Pixie's urge to sun herself in cars that finished the relationship.

One evening, the cat did not come home at bedtime. The couple presumes she'd crawled through the open window of the car and that the owners had driven away without noticing her.

"We cried for a week," Marion admitted.

About a week after Pixie's disappearance, Marion and Ernie were in bed for the night when they felt the presence of their beloved cat jump up on the bed. Then they felt her snuggle in to her accustomed sleeping position.

"This continued for about a year and a half," Marion remembered. "Eventually her visits became less frequent and then not at all. Where she really was during those nightly visits we'll never know."

Another question might be: Were the Clarkes or Pixie providing the comfort?

18: The Meredith Tale

There's not much Edmontonians cherish more than a fine spring day. The harshness of the winter makes the glory of spring much more appreciated than it would be in less severe climates. Perhaps this enjoyment was even more intense for the earliest European settlers. They had few of the amenities that we take for granted now.

The spring of 1892 brought sunshine, clear skies and two beautiful young women to Edmonton. Elizabeth and Isobel Osler's uncle had founded the town of South Edmonton just a few years before. The girls were a delightful addition to the fledgling town. Not only were they strikingly beautiful, but the sisters were talented musicians as well.

Predictably in this pioneering community, men outnumbered women by a goodly number, and the sisters' status soon changed from spinsters to wives. Isobel's husband, Arthur Meredith, "the scion of a distinguished Toronto family," had come west to seek his fortune. It seems he was successful in this because he was able to build a lovely home on a hill just off what is, today, Calgary Trail Southbound.

Isobel and Arthur were blessed with two sons. Their lives seemed to be unfolding as they'd planned. Sadly, appearances were deceiving. Arthur Meredith died suddenly, "without warning and apparently for no cause, almost as if he had stopped living by an act of will," according to Tony Cashman's story.

The young widow took her husband's remains and her two sons and returned to the east. Sister Elizabeth and her family followed shortly. Not one member of the once-happy and productive families remained in the area.

The Meredith residence stood vacant for a time. Oddly, considering the house had been lived in with love and joy, no one seemed very comfortable about going into it or even near it. A young man named Billy Wilkin was charged with the responsibility of looking after the place.

Billy heard of a family who had just arrived in the Edmonton area from Michigan. It was early December and bitterly cold. The immigrant family, twenty-four in all, had brought a load of personal belongings, but no money. Billy Wilkin offered the use of the Meredith place to the destitute immigrants, rent free, while they established themselves. Gratefully, they accepted.

Surprisingly, a week later, two of the men from the Michigan family arrived at Billy Wilkin's door and announced they would have to vacate the house. It was haunted, they reported.

A practical man, Billy felt this was a matter that only required a little investigation. He and two fellow businessmen, Harry Perry and a grocer named McIntyre, travelled out to the estate that evening. They found the family in a highly distraught state. They were quite clearly a badly frightened lot.

Tony Cashman quotes Billy Wilkin as saying, "... exactly at nine o'clock there came the most terrific rap on the back door. It sounded as if a drunken man was trying to get in. The three of us immediately rushed to the door. We opened it but found no sign of anyone. There was a full moon, with six inches of snow on the ground, and it was almost as light as day. McIntyre stayed in the door while Perry went around to one side of the house and I the other, meeting again at the back door. There was no sign of anyone and no tracks in the snow. We went back into the house, feeling rather mystified, but thought possibly some joker might be monkeying around."

Not long after that, the investigators heard someone walking on the floor of the attic above.

"It was so clear that you could trace it. It seemed to be about two feet from the wall. It was impossible for anyone to walk there because the house had a cottage roof, and at that point it was only three feet high."

The trio decided the attic would have to be searched. As soon as they opened the trap door, the sound stopped immediately. Armed with lanterns, the three men stayed in the attic as long as they could, waiting for the sounds to recur. Approximately half an hour lapsed and nothing had happened. The men were "half frozen" by then and they climbed back down. In a few minutes, the noises started up again.

Thinking that rodents might be the cause of the commotion, the men spread flour across the attic floor. The noises started again as soon as they'd climbed back down. Hoping to find tracks through the flour, the men went into the frigid attic for a third time. The flour lay untouched and by seven o'clock the following morning the men left, mystified.

The family from Michigan gamely tried to stay on in their free accommodation but fled a few nights later during a blizzard. They had decided that paying rent for a house with fewer attributes was preferable to staying where the Merediths had once lived. Many tenants followed but none stayed. All had similar frightening experiences.

The old house stood empty till 1910, when Mr. and Mrs. Harry Sandeman temporarily took possession of the place. The couple had just arrived from England. They agreed that there certainly were some unusual sounds but they were not bothered by them. In England, sharing your home with a ghost was not considered reason to panic. It was not even seen as undesirable.

The Sandemans were the last people to live in the house. Then it sat empty and, over the years that followed, fell into disrepair. The Meredith homestead that had once been a scene of laughter, love, and happiness eventually fell victim to progress and was torn down. Today a rental townhouse project, Huntington Hill, sits on that same site.

This story appears courtesy Tony Cashman, an Edmonton historian and author. The tale is included in his book *The Best of Edmonton Stories*.

19: Departed Husband Visits

One beautiful spring day I was hanging laundry out on the line and watching my neighbour, Mary Werstiuk, tending to her annual vegetable garden. Although we don't know each other well, Mary's garden has become a standard family topic in our house of non-gardeners. Consistently, the lady produces corn, zucchinis, carrots, and all manner of other fresh vegetables of virtually prize-winning size and abundance.

"Steroids," we would joke, as year after year we watched this incredible green thumb turn out bumper crops.

On this particular day, Mary made a strange comment to me:

"My husband's around again." What seemed odd was that I thought I remembered her telling me sometime ago that she'd been a widow for a number of years.

"What do you mean?" I asked.

"It happens every year when I put in my garden," Mary replied, indicating a large area of newly planted vegetables. "He and my mother both come around and watch me. This used to be my mother's house. She always had a garden and she loved it. After Bill and I moved here we kept it up; Bill really enjoyed it. Now they're both gone, but they still come around every spring."

"What makes you say that?" I asked.

"I can feel them for one thing. But that's not all. Every year I plan out my garden. I decide that one vegetable would be best here or that I'll have more or fewer rows of another kind. It's all clear in my head when I start, but by the time I've finished I've done the garden exactly the way we always did when Mom and Bill were alive."

"Does this only happen when you're gardening?" I wondered.

She explained that her husband actually visits her fairly frequently.

"How can you be sure it's him?" I persisted.

"Well, for one thing, Bill was always a terrible tease. Take these shoes, for instance."

Mary held up a pair of perfectly ordinary looking white sneakers. "I washed these last night and put them out on the back steps to dry. One of them is completely dry and the other is still soaking wet. That's the sort of prank Bill would just love to pull."

Bill's last gift to Mary was a pair of earrings. "They weren't particularly expensive ones, but I treasured them. They were on my dresser when I went to bed one night and in the morning they were gone. I vacuumed the house completely and then emptied the vacuum bag looking for them. They weren't there. All of my kids came over to help look. We searched the whole house and even vacuumed again but we didn't turn them up. So, I gave them up for lost. Then about six months later, there they were on my dresser exactly where they'd been when I'd last seen them. I know they couldn't have been there all along. Bill had them, I'm sure."

I was curious about Mary's emotional reaction to being visited by those who are no longer living.

"Oh, no. They don't frighten me. I feel good knowing they're around looking after me," she replied calmly.

"Have you ever seen them, or do you just feel their presence?" I inquired.

It seems Mary has learned how to see her husband. Initially, she would wake in the night with a startled feeling that someone was staring at her. "I'd sit right up and open my eyes wide. There'd be no one there."

Eventually she became somewhat used to the sensation and was able to control her reactions. "If I just lie there calmly and slowly open my eyes I can see Bill standing beside my bed. I used to try going toward him but he would hold his arm out, with the palm of his hand facing me. That pretty clearly told me to stop, that he didn't want me approaching him."

His widow is not the only family member Bill visits on a regular basis.

"Our son Jim knows his father is around frequently, too. Bill was always very proud of his kids, especially when they all bought houses. He just loved Jim's house."

Unfortunately, sometime after his father's death, Jim's marriage broke up and the young man had to sell the house. As a real-estate agent who had been showing the place to prospective buyers was leaving, he assured Jim all the basement lights were turned out. Despite this, Jim noticed a glare coming from the basement and went down to check. Not only were all the lights on but the centre fixture was hanging down three feet lower than it should have been. Neither the agent nor his clients remember there being anything unusual about the recreation room light fixture, but they do clearly remember having turned off all the lights.

"I'm sure that was Bill," Mary said. "He didn't want Jim to sell the place."

Despite his dead father's best efforts, the house did sell and moving day came. That morning, Jim noticed that the doors on his china cabinet were open. He closed them and went about packing the few remaining articles in the house. As he passed by the cabinet again, he was surprised to see that the doors were open again. Jim had owned this piece of furniture for several years, and the doors had to be tugged to pull open. By the time he'd closed them three or four times, Jim realized his father was trying to get his attention.

"If you want to come, crawl in then, Dad," Jim suggested. The china cabinet doors have never given him a moment's trouble since.

Did Bill follow his son? Recently, Jim and his second wife have moved into a newly built home.

"They have mirrored doors on their closet," Mary explained. "Heather, Jim's wife, had never met Bill. One day she was sitting on the edge of her bed and she saw the image of a man in the closet door. 'I wonder if that's Bill,' she thought. When Jim got home that night, Heather told him about the experience and described the man she'd seen in the mirror. Sure enough it was Bill."

Did he ride to Jim's new residence in the china cabinet? One can only guess, but certainly the dead man's presence cannot be denied.

20: Bedroom in Bedroom Community is Haunted

As a result of its proximity to Edmonton, the town of Beaumont has, in recent years, become a bedroom community. Despite its present-day role, the community does have a long and proud heritage as one of the earliest areas to be settled in northern Alberta.

A few years ago the Harris family bought a house in Beaumont. With four children under the age of six to raise, Mr. and Mrs. Harris were concerned about finding a suitable place to settle in.

A serene and quiet quality of life for all six of them was of prime importance. After months of diligent house hunting, first an area and then a specific house was chosen. All members of the family old enough to voice an opinion were delighted with the choice. This was truly going to be home, everyone agreed.

Not long after they'd moved, the mother heard crying from the baby's bedroom. She went up immediately to see what was the matter. Surprisingly, she found the baby sleeping soundly and contentedly. As the puzzled woman stood by the crib, the bedroom door closed. This startled her, but as there was nothing wrong with her child the woman left the room.

Night after night, the scenario was repeated. The three older children and their father also heard the crying. Each time they checked the nursery and found the child fast asleep. The family was beginning to change their minds about the appropriateness of this particular house and even the town as a good place to be trying to settle in. At last, in frantic desperation, the couple contacted a psychic who agreed to come out and assess the strange situation.

Her first impression was a distinct and dramatic one. She felt that there was a child's spirit stranded in the house. The psychic instructed it to leave. That night there was no crying but there were loud noises and doors banging closed for no apparent reason.

Several nights later, the young mother dreamed of an angry man walking down the hall and going into the nursery. In her dream he disappeared into the closet. A woman was sitting in a rocking chair near the closet and she spoke to the dreaming mother and, and in a voice filled with hate, accused her: "You took my baby."

Badly shaken by the dream the woman got up and busied herself until morning. As soon as it was a reasonable hour to make a phone call, the frightened young mother got in touch with the psychic.

The woman came out directly. She sat quietly for a prolonged period in the nursery. In time it became clear to the psychic that during her first visit only the spirit of the baby had been released. The child's distraught parents remained in the Harris's home.

The psychic gave the same instructions to the parents that she had to the child's spirit. They must have found their precious infant because there were never any more unexplained sounds in the Harris's house. They live there to this day and are happily raising their family in the calm and loving atmosphere they'd always hoped to. Presumably, the family that once haunted the Harris's lives and home is also calm and happy since their reunion.

Calgary Ghost
Stories

21: Price Paid
for Checkered Past

There must be truth in the saying, "It's all in what you're used to." Most people would be badly shaken if they went to work and saw a ghost. However, for employees of the Deane House and Tea Room on the grounds of Fort Calgary, seeing ghosts is pretty well included in their duty roster. As a matter of fact, the Deane House might well hold bragging rights to the title "Alberta's Most Haunted Place." Given the residence's checkered past, the standing is quite understandable.

The Deane House was built in 1906 as the official residence for Royal North West Mounted Police Superintendent Richard Burton Deane, his wife and their five children. Mrs. Deane died that year and neither she nor any of her children ever lived in the house.

Today the residence is the only building remaining from what was once a busy garrison. It has been designated an historic site and is enjoyed by many as both a period museum and a unique stop for a light lunch, but the years since 1906 have not been quiet ones at the Deane House.

In 1914 the house was moved to the southeast of its original location. The Grand Trunk Pacific Railway had purchased the building with the intention of using it as the station master's home.

In 1929 the Deane House was moved again, this time to its present site, across the Elbow River. This second move was considered an engineering curiosity and was reported on in the magazine *Popular Mechanics*.

More than the location was changed with this move. The new owner, C. L. Jacques, renovated the interior and the once-grand RCMP residence became the Gaspé Lodge Boarding House. It remained a boarding house for the better part of four decades. During those years, the house was the site of an inordinate number of deaths, many of them violent.

In the 1920s a man died after being pushed down the staircase. After that, there were two suicides, a prostitute was murdered there, a young woman jumped to her death from one of the Deane House windows, a man was gunned down on the home's porch, and a man died of natural causes while sitting in the parlour. The most grizzly deaths were the strangulation murder of a mother and the suicide of her husband while their children watched.

In 1973 the City of Calgary purchased the property and it was used as an artists' and authors' co-operative and studio until 1978 when it received Historic Resource Designation. The building was restored on the first floor to resemble what it would have originally looked like. A section of the main floor has become a delightful Tea House. Fittingly, a tea-leaf reader is available to do readings for lunch guests.

Atez Jackci has worked as a waiter in the Tea House for five years. He obviously enjoys his job immensely and has won awards recognizing his skill as a waiter. He's also well aware of just how haunted the building is.

"Oh, yes," the quiet spoken young man confirmed. "I've seen them. I'm not the only one. Most of the staff have had experiences."

Atez has clearly been exposed to more incidents than anyone else on staff. The Tea Room is immediately to the left of the front entrance.

"We often hear laughter from the front foyer. When we check, there's no one there."

The study on the opposite side of the entranceway has been redone to reflect how it might have looked as Captain Deane's study. During the years as the Gaspé Lodge, a man died of natural causes in that room. The man's image is often visible. He sits comfortably in a chair in the study. The ghost never disturbs anyone, he just sits smoking his pipe.

In keeping with the theme of Deane's study, an antique telephone sits on a secretary-style desk. The phone is only an ornament. It has no inner workings and is not hooked up to any power source. Despite this, the telephone will occasionally ring. Atez smiles as he recalls staff members who were new at the time being startled by the phenomenon. Veteran staff just go about their work, confident in their assumption that the call is no concern of theirs.

Spooky goings-on in the Deane House are certainly not limited to noises. Atez explained: "I watched a man walk down the stairs. His image was very solid, but he was cut off at the knees. He was dressed in a black cloak and hat, in a fashion that looked to be from about the late 1920s. I'd estimate his age at 36. He walked down the stairs, through the foyer, past me and out the front door. He didn't seem to notice me."

A glass cabinet that once sat in the parlour has recently had to be re-

At Deane House, the unconnected, antique phone on the desk occasionally rings, and a presence has been seen in the chair.

moved for safety purposes. On several occasions and for no apparent reason, the glass has flown out and shattered. Because there seemed to be no way to prevent or even predict this dangerous occurrence, the cabinet has been moved from the house.

On Friday evenings the Deane House hosts murder-mystery dinners. Local actors stage a murder while interacting with the guests. Once the murder has been committed, it is up to the guests to determine "who dunnit." The evenings are very popular.

"We ask the guests not to go down to the basement. We explain that none of the clues are there. It's only a staff preparation area. Well, one lady decided not to pay any attention to this and went downstairs anyway. She came back up just bent right out of shape. She told me that some old Indian with long braids had told her she shouldn't be down there, that the area was sacred. She wanted me to go down and tell the guy off. Well, I did go down there, but, of course, there was no one there."

Atez spoke with utter calm of these strange experiences.

"I had a very positive experience as a child. I saw my grandmother after she'd died. It was so comforting that I think, since then, I've been open to the idea of ghosts."

In one instance, though, Atez did flee in terror from the Deane House.

"The place was closed in the summer of 1990. I was here alone. I heard footsteps coming down the stairs. They were extremely heavy and they really scared me. I was sure something was coming to get me. I dropped what I was doing, turned on the motion detectors and ran out into the yard. It took a long time for me to calm down. When I did and went back into the house, the motion detectors hadn't registered anything."

Despite his predominantly "matter of fact" outlook, Atez readily admits working there hasn't always been easy.

"There have been days when it's just been too draining to be here. The odd time I've just had to pack it in and go home."

That hasn't happened recently, though, because in April of 1990, the Deane House was exorcised.

"The psychic who did the exorcism knew everything about the place. It was uncanny," Atez reported.

The day after the exorcism proved to be a real challenge for employees at the Deane House.

"It was unreal. Electrical appliances would start and stop working for no apparent reason; the clocks would read the wrong time. It was so difficult to work that several people went home early."

Since then there have been no more ghosts seen or heard. The exorcism cleaned the stately residence out of all paranormal phenomena. All except one.

The attic of the Deane House remains pretty well as it was originally. Typical of most attics, the windows are dormer style. On each side of the window facing the Fort Calgary site, there are storage closets. The one on the right hand side is full of paraphernalia needed for the school programs the House hosts. The one on the left hand side remains empty.

Fort Calgary Communications Coordinator, Kerklan Hilton, explained, "The spirits don't like us to store anything in this closet. They became very agitated and so we respect their wishes."

Strange that it's that particular closet: it looks exactly like the other one – well, maybe not exactly. On the floor of the empty closet, there's a deep red stain that years of cleaning haven't ever been able to remove.

22: Anniversary Walk?

Calgarians will remember 1988 as the year their city hosted the Winter Olympics. It was a dramatic, colourful and successful time for Calgary citizens. Jan Nahornick, her mother and her daughter are among those with vivid recollections – and it is a day in August of that same year that the three ladies remember best: August 5th.

"We had been to a family reunion in Drumheller," the personable Jan explained. "We visited in Lethbridge, too, and then headed home for Calgary."

In order to complete what had been a full "family" weekend, Jan, her mother and daughter decided go to Queen's Park cemetery, where her father is buried.

"We felt we wanted to pay our respects and we always like to keep the grave looking nice, too," she explained.

They drove into the grounds at 5:20 p.m. The normally busy cemetery appeared to have no visitors for the moment. The gravesite they were visiting was up on a knoll and has a clear view of the area around it. There were no other cars or people to be seen.

"My daughter went to fill a jug we had in the car, to water the flowers on Dad's grave," Jan continued. "Mom and I stayed in the car and were just looking around and enjoying the peace and quiet. There was no one around. Then, out of nowhere, there was someone – a woman in a beige, long-sleeved, flowing dress. She had beautiful hair and was wearing a pearl necklace, but she was empty handed. She wasn't carrying a purse."

As it would most women, the lack of purse struck Jan and her mother as being extremely odd.

"My daughter saw her, too, and thought it was very strange that the lady would be walking up by the headstones. Also, the way she was walking was unusual. She was almost waltzing."

Not surprisingly, the ladies were fascinated by the unique sight and watched her intently. Despite their curiosity, Jan added, "We all got the feeling that this was something we weren't supposed to be watching."

The apparition paused at a particular headstone. Jan had already started their car and was driving toward the headstone that the woman with the pearl necklace had stopped at.

"All I had to do was turn the car around. I've timed it since and this lady was only out of our sight for one minute and thirteen seconds. By the time we were facing in her direction again, she was gone. Vanished. Nowhere to be seen." Jan paused in her story. "You must remember we were up on a hill and could see all around the cemetery. This lady was just plain no longer there."

In case the woman might have been hidden because she was kneeling down behind the headstone, the family drove to the place they'd last seen the mysterious woman. There was no one. The entire cemetery remained as empty as when they'd driven in. Puzzled, the three stared at the headstone in front of them. Below the lady's name to whom the monument had been erected was a record of the date she'd died. August 5th. Perhaps the lady's spirit was taking an anniversary stroll.

23: The House with an Evil Spirit

Some of the most ordinary houses can have most extraordinary pasts. A dramatic history can have a profound influence on a building's future. One ghastly occurrence can set the stage for years of unhappiness. This is the pattern in the following story. The haunted house is like all the neighbouring ones in appearance, but the events that have tainted it have now spilled over into surrounding homes. Apparently this is too ugly a possession to be contained in one small house.

In 1948, a corpse was found that partially solved a nearly twenty-year-old mystery. Cecil Pearce had just bought a house in the Capitol Hill area of Calgary. For undocumented reasons he had the basement excavated and made a horrible discovery. There, lying below Pearce's real-estate investment, was the body of Thomas C. Hall, who had owned the house when he disappeared in March of 1929. The soil had preserved the body in a semi-mummified and readily identifiable state.

Hall had apparently been murdered by an opponent in a game of cards. Unfortunately, police were never able to prove this theory, and no one was ever charged with the murder.

We can assume that Pearce was not delighted by the discovery of his subterranean tenant, but he could not have been totally surprised by it either. For some time, he'd been listening to complaints by his three daughters about "feeling a mysterious clammy hand" poking at them.

Even then, they were concerned enough to begin an investigation into the history of the home. During this research, they discovered that a previous owner, Elizabeth Irish, often complained of, what seemed at the time, an irrational uneasiness in the house.

The Pearce and the Irish families were not the only ones to be aware of strange goings-on. Rick Passey, who owned the house in 1982, recalled hearing unexplained knockings at the front door.

Oddly, the peculiar reports were not restricted to that particular house but also diffused through the surrounding dwellings. Neighbours nearby had long accepted that there was "something unnatural" about the nondescript bungalow.

Edith Taylor, a long-time area resident, recalled that shortly after the discovery of the body, horrific tragedy struck the neighbourhood. Families in the three houses closest to Hall's all suffered the death of a child. Hall's ghost was also generally blamed for seemingly higher-than-normal family instability in the surrounding area. Living in or even near this particular house, it seemed, had brought bad luck to any who tried it, even after the unfortunate Mr. Hall's corpse was removed.

Hopefully, the spirit of Thomas Hall has somehow been avenged by now. The hope that the man's soul is at peace is probably nowhere more deeply cherished than in his old house, because, at this writing, that malevolent residence is still occupied.

Perhaps if anyone is looking for a new home, some investigation beyond the normal parameters of real-estate listings might be insurance of a peaceful future.

24: Is Stately Residence Home to a Ghost?

Many haunted places have unusual histories. The truth of this could lead one to ask the question: which is cause and which is effect. Are these places haunted because of all that has gone on in them over the years, or is all the unusual activity a result of a ghostly presence?

The Coste House in Calgary certainly fits into this "which came first" dilemma. The home, a twenty-eight-room mansion, is located in the Mount Royal section of Calgary, a neighbourhood that historian Jack Peach describes as "mansion-rich."

Eugene Coste, the original owner and resident, built the house in 1913 with profits from natural gas exploration. Coste and his wife lived in the mansion for nine years and then returned to their native Quebec. As the Costes were childless, one would have to suppose they enjoyed their privacy. The home has ten-foot ceilings, a conservatory, reception areas of "baronial proportions," a sweeping main staircase, many stone-rimmed French windows, thirteen gas-burning fireplaces, a "regal portico" over the main entrance, and two and a half acres of exquisite landscaping.

When the Costes left Calgary, they offered the mansion to the city, but as both the property and the tax assessment it carried were enormous, the city fathers turned down Eugene Coste's generous offer. Clearly, money was not an obstacle with the Costes because they moved away without selling the valuable property. It stood empty for years and the unpaid taxes accumulated against it. By the 1930s, the City of Calgary had, thanks to back taxes, what they'd turned down a few years before.

The next tenants in the rambling home were the art and dressmaking departments of the Provincial Institute of Technology and Art. This group, the forerunner to the Allied Arts Centre, happily occupied and fully utilized the mansion from 1946 to 1959.

Calgary historian Peach reported, "The fine old place was filled with the noises of theatrical groups, weavers' looms, potters' wheels, metal workers' hammers, and earnestly practising instrumentalists and singers."

A gentleman named Archie Key was the Institute's director. He lived at the house and was kept from being lonely by one Dr. Carmichael, the Coste House ghost. How or why Dr. Carmichael resided there is undetermined. It was apparently remembered by some that the Costes left an attendant in the house when they moved back east. Those people presume that this is the apparition that Archie saw so frequently. Others use the standard Alberta-ghost theory that the house had been built on an ancient Indian burial ground. How the latter would account for a ghost of European descent raises more questions than it answers.

Despite his unknown origin, Dr. Carmichael was frequently seen "drifting through darkened rooms, hallways and on the central staircase," according to Jack Peach. After chats with Archie about the ghost, Jack reported that the presence alternately frightened and then comforted Archie.

In 1959, the Allied Arts Centre moved out of the Coste House. Although ownership of the property changed in the next few years, the place remained empty until it was purchased by Robert and Mary Lamond.

Bob Lamond reported that he "bought it for a song" and has since restored the place to its original grandeur. The Lamonds and their two children enjoy living in the enormous home, perhaps especially so because Dr. Carmichael's ghost evidently moved out before they moved in.

Mrs. Lamond stated categorically, "For us the house is not haunted."

Perhaps the stability of family life has, by now, made up for the years of abandonment and varied occupants.

25: Calgary Firehalls: "They're All Haunted"

The City of Calgary Fire Department referred my inquiry about haunted firehalls to Frank Silliker, president of the Fire Department Museum Society. After introducing myself on the phone I told Frank the reason for my call: "I've heard that a couple of former firehalls in Calgary are haunted."

The man chuckled and replied, "They're all haunted."

U nfortunately, there's not much documentation for "all" the stations but, exaggeration aside, Mr. Silliker was able to provide details for three different locations. With one exception, it is horses, not people, that are responsible for the hauntings.

The horses, of course, were an integral part of the fire-fighting team in the early years of this century. Their names have even been recorded in the archival records of the Calgary Fire Department. Bob, Browny, Jimmy, Squibby, Senator L, or Joe Booth might well be the animals whose spirits remain in three former firehalls.

It seemed that the animals took their careers as seriously as the men did. Frank explained, "As soon as the horses heard the bell, they would leave the stalls and go to their places in front of the wagons."

By the early 1930s, the entire force was motorized and the animals that remained were retired. Apparently, at least some of them were very at-

The Phantom Lounge is out of business, but the old firehall's inhabitants (human or animal) may not have departed.

tached to their exciting life on the fire-fighting team and were not ready to be put out to pasture.

The station at 1110 Memorial Drive North West was built in 1906 and served as a firehall until 1964. Today, the City of Calgary Parks department uses some space on the main floor, and a canoe club rents part of the area upstairs.

"I've been told by people who have worked alone in the building that occasionally they hear the sound of a bell ringing in the distance. Right after the bell sounds, they say they can hear commotion from the first floor. They say it sounds like an echo of horses whinnying and hooves on a cement floor."

Maintenance people, tenants in the building over the past years, and even people walking on the path behind the old firehall have reported hearing these noises.

The ghosts of former firehall #3 are not as easily identified. The building still stands at 1030 9th Avenue South East. It served as a firehall from 1906 to 1952. Until recently, the Firehall Restaurant occupied the building.

No one has ever been able to determine whether it's men or horses who haunt the building. Over the years though, many people have reported hearing strange, unexplained noises and experiencing unusual feelings in the place.

Budget Rent A Car now occupies the old #1 station at 138 6th Avenue South East, which was built in 1911 and used as a firehall until 1973.

Historian Silliker explained: "A firefighter named N. Cocks (his first name may have been Norman) was killed in the station on May 8, 1962, during a drill. He's still around, there's no denying it."

The horses haven't left the station either. Even today the distinct sounds of horses moving around and the clatter of their hooves on the cement floor can occasionally be heard. Frank cannot explain why so many firehalls in the province are haunted except to suggest, "There were some very dedicated people. It seems some can never go to their rest. As long as the building exists, they'll be there."

Frank Silliker has taken steps to ensure the buildings will remain for the ghosts and the living to enjoy. They are all protected as provincial historic sites.

26: The Lady Required
Lots of Attention

The question of whether it's people or places that are haunted is complicated further by this story. Of all the employees of Fort Calgary's haunted Deane House, Atez Jackci has been witness to the greatest number of sightings. Long before he worked there, Atez lived in a haunted apartment.

T he elegant female apparition was clearly not a figment of Atez's imagination. On several occasions, his room-mates and guests felt her presence.

"The apartment had both a front and back door," the personable young man explained. "Many people who came to visit would ask that we leave both doors open. They felt this dead woman's presence, and somehow having the doors open made them feel easier about visiting."

The apartment is located in Mount Royal, an elegant and older area of Calgary.

"The Congress is the name of the building I lived in. There's an identical one next to it. They were built for older people who were moving out of their mansions in that area."

Presumably the ghost in Atez's suite was one of the original tenants.

Guests may have been leery of the part-time lady resident in the suite,

The Congress apartment block, located in the Mount Royal area of Calgary, was home to at least one non-paying resident of the "spiritual" persuasion.

but Atez and his roommates were not. They did, on occasion, find her a bit much to deal with.

"She needed a lot of attention and she would make it known when she wasn't happy. We always knew when she was arriving. The pipes sounded as if they were going to explode. We often felt her in the corner of the dining room; that's the only room I ever saw her in."

This sighting is a strange one because the apartment wasn't rented to Atez furnished. He brought his own furniture into the suite and the one time Atez did see the ghost, she was sitting at his dining room table.

"She was an older woman and very elegantly dressed. She was wearing a pill-box hat with a veil. She looked very proper."

Atez was very aware of her presence whenever the ghost was in the apartment. There's no question in his mind that this was the woman he and his guests had been sensing.

Frequently, when Atez or his roommates would come home, they would hear music coming from inside their apartment.

"It was music from the 1930s or '40s. Then, when we'd open the door, the sounds would stop and there was no one there."

The woman could be a real nuisance when she set her mind to it.

"She'd turn the stove on and off when you were cooking. Once, when I was in the bathroom, I heard someone knocking on the door. There was no one there."

The apartment was heated by gas, and because it was so large, Atez and his roommates quickly fell into the habit of leaving the gas furnace on at all times.

"One time I came home and it was ice cold in the apartment. I know the furnace had been on when I left, but it was turned off when I returned. I figured it would take quite awhile for the place to warm up so I went to get the matches to light the furnace right away. By the time I got back, the furnace was lit and the apartment was comfortably warm."

The ghostly woman did not stay in the suite all the time. When she was there, though, Atez found it best to acknowledge her arrival.

"One morning I knew she'd come in. The pipes were making an awful racket. I was alone and tired. I just didn't want to bother with her, so I stayed in bed. Then I heard three crashes and I got up to investigate."

A china figurine of Charlie Chaplin lay in pieces on the dining room floor, across the room from the shelf where it had been displayed.

"She must have thrown it. I had it out with her then. I told her not to break anything of mine ever again," Atez remembered. "I was able to repair the broken doll and after that she seemed to work through it. People complained that Charlie Chaplin's eyes leered at them and would follow them wherever they went in the apartment."

Not long after the broken-doll incident, Atez moved upstairs in The Congress to a smaller suite.

"I wondered if she would come with me. One day, when I was coming down the staircase I was thinking about her, and as I reached out my hand to put it on the newel post, the staircase extended and then retracted itself. I guess that was her way of letting me know she was still around."

Since then, Atez has moved to another area of the city. He was distressed to read of a murder in The Congress in the summer of 1991.

"I understand it may have taken place in my old apartment."

To this day Atez wonders if the woman's presence that he had come to know so well might have been a contributing factor in the death.

27: A Dog Breathing Down Your Neck

In 1975 Nicky Bellerose was working in a Calgary art shop. The business was located in an old house in the southwest of the city, at 823 6 Avenue South West. She only stayed employed there for six months, and the shop has since closed, but it's an experience that Nicky will never forget.

While I was touring the Prince House in Calgary's Heritage Park, Nicky overheard my conversation with a park interpreter. She approached me right away.

"I couldn't help hearing what you said. I've had an experience you might be interested in. If you think you want to include my story, just give me a call," the pretty, dark-haired woman advised.

Before the weekend was over, I had spoken with Nicky, at length. Her story is a most unusual one, even for a ghost story.

In order to "set the stage" for sharing her experience, Nicky explained that the employees at the art shop commonly accepted that the building was haunted.

"The motion detectors would go off at odd times when apparently no one had triggered them," she recalled. "The owners had people in to inspect the alarm device and the building's wiring, but nothing was ever found."

The unproductive inspections did nothing to relieve the owners' or employees' apprehensions: the phantom alarms continued. Further inspectors were called in when strong and very localized smells began being noted in various spots around the building.

"There was one particularly strong odour in the foyer. We never figured out what caused it and were never able to get rid of it." Nicky added, "There was another, different smell just at the top of the basement stairs, and others would just occur in different spots for different lengths of time."

Gas inspectors were called in to investigate, but no problems were found. One particular smell is one Nicky will never forget.

"It made me feel really uncomfortable," she remembered. "I was kneeling down, bending over some work. I felt and smelled the hot breath of a dog behind me, breathing on the back of my neck and my ear. A dog's breath is pretty distinctive. I'm sure that's what it was."

That last experience had a hand in Nicky's decision to move along in her career.

"I've always intended to go back and see what's there now. I'd like to ask some questions but up till now I haven't been able to do it," Nicky confessed.

As Nicky still lives in Calgary and appears to be a highly motivated and energetic person it is neither geography nor laziness that has kept her from completing the intended mission. It sounds suspiciously like one of those plans we all have that we'd just as soon not carry out. Or perhaps it's the other way around. Perhaps it's the will of the spirits preventing Nicky from fulfilling her long-standing goal. Perhaps the spirits wish to be undisturbed by the current tenants in the building, to be left alone.

28: Opera House
Alive With Spirits

Alberta's settlers may have had hard lives, but they knew how to enjoy themselves. The existence of the Canmore Opera House is proof of that. Built in the small mining community around the turn of the century, the Opera House was designed for the purpose it's named for, as well as a rehearsal and concert hall.

You would be hard pressed to find a less interesting building from an architectural perspective, but what it lacks in design style, the House definitely makes up in a distinctly colourful past and even present.

Years after its life in the performing arts, the nondescript building was called into service as a hospital and then as a retirement home for local coal miners. By 1960 the historic site sat empty and deteriorating. Fortunately, it was identified as an important part of the area's heritage and was moved, in 1966, to Calgary's Heritage Park. Today it is on display as a museum, but it is also used as a functioning theatre.

A park interpreter explained that the old and beautiful grand piano which sits on the Opera House stage can periodically be heard playing while no one is near it. She's also been told of costumes being strewn around dressing rooms while the building was "empty."

"I've never had any experiences myself," she explained. "But I still don't

Productions in the old Canmore Opera House may be watched by musically gifted ghosts.

like going into the auditorium by myself. Maybe it's just that it's dark but it really is creepy." Vera Burns, a former park employee, reported that actors with different troupes had complained of hearing loud footsteps and party-like sounds of voices and dinnerware clanking.

Over the years a number of people have reported seeing the ghost of a man sitting contentedly in the auditorium and watching the stage. Vera explained that the ghost has definite preferences for certain performances. She is quoted in the January 25, 1982, edition of *Alberta Report* as saying, "He likes musicals best and can be seen looking over the crowd when we have one."

Some park staff believe he's the ghost of a patron from the 1897 to 1913 era and that he's returned to enjoy the Canmore Band, which played in the Opera House at that time. Others are sure it's the ghost of Sam Livingston, an area pioneer, whose original homestead has also been moved to Heritage Park. Interestingly, a presence that was distinctly adult and distinctly male was felt in that house as well.

It may never be known whether it is, in fact, Sam who haunts the Canmore Opera House. Although the Livingston homestead has always been and still is located close to where the Opera House has sat for twenty-five years, it is just as reasonable to speculate that the ghost is the spirit of a long-deceased miner with an undying love of music and performance.

What certainly can be attested to is that the Opera House is haunted. This premise is accepted as fact by anyone who has worked in or around it for any length of time. Whoever haunts the House has not left it with a jubilant atmosphere. As dreary as the exterior appearance of the building is, the ambience inside is even more bleak and joyless.

Like the park interpreter, I wondered if the melancholy feeling in the theatre was caused only by the requisite darkness; but my suspicions tell me it's more than that. Through all my explorations, I've come to associate the damp, cool feeling that this building has with a ghost.

29: Rugged Sam Stays With His House

The Sam Livingston house, in Calgary's Heritage Park, was a very busy place when it was new. Sam, his wife, Jane, and their fourteen children shared it with the local school teacher and his wife as well as any travellers who were in need of temporary accommodation.

Sam was a colourful character around whom many tales have been woven. Heritage Park interpreter Reta Anderson recounts a legend that speaks volumes for the late Livingston's personality.

"He was out on the trap lines with his dog, and his return home was delayed by a severe storm. Sam had run out of food some days before, and he knew that if he didn't get something to eat, he would die while he waited out the storm. What did he do? He cut off his dog's tail. He made soup for himself and gave the bones to the dog."

That's as pragmatic as a person can be. It certainly fits his character that he would be back to his old homestead periodically, to make sure everything was being handled to his liking.

Reta explained further: "One day in August 1990 a lady came through to see the house. We weren't busy; it was the middle of the week and late in the season. I was showing the visitor around upstairs when both of us realized we weren't alone. We could both feel the presence of another

83

Sam and Jane Livingston's house in Heritage Park dates from about 1865. He may have stayed on.

human being. We mentioned it to each other and agreed it was an adult male.

"He accompanied us down the stairs and stood with us for awhile as we were talking by the door. Then, as quickly as he had joined us, he left. Not very polite, was he?" she added rhetorically.

Reta reported that neither she nor the visitor were frightened by the sensation, although she's often thought of the incident since and wondered whether or not the presence was, in fact, Sam.

30: Beautiful Woman in White

The Prince House is a grand, old, three-storey place built of sturdy yellow bricks. The building was moved from its original site in 1966 to the grounds of Heritage Park. The move was a mammoth undertaking that required the house to be hauled in three separate sections. Despite the upheaval, the house arrived at Heritage Park complete with its ghost.

Rick Smith, general manager of the unique Calgary park/museum, explained that a couple of seasons ago interpreters in the house were shocked to hear about the beautiful woman in the white dress holding the baby in one of the upstairs bedrooms. When they investigated, the room was as empty as they expected it should be.

One visitor was perturbed enough by what she had seen that some months later she was still not able to get the incident out of her mind, and she contacted the park. The lady described in detail the exquisite beauty of the woman holding the baby. She had been wearing a gown so white it virtually cast a glow, and when she had smiled at the lady and her companions, an atmosphere of peace spread throughout the room.

That sighting was certainly the most dramatic report the park staff had ever had from Prince House, but reported sightings of the mother and child have come to be expected by now.

One incident that Rick Smith did not expect, and hopes never to have repeated, was a call from park security one morning, at 2:30 a.m. They wanted to let him know there were lights on in the third floor of Prince House. Rick knew that was impossible because the third floor was closed off and had been for years. Besides, there was no electricity to that storey. The guard was insistent, however, and Rick eventually had to leave his home and drive to meet the worried guard.

Sure enough, the entire third floor of the large house was lit. Initially Rick assumed that it was merely a reflection from the lights across the lake. That, unfortunately, would not explain the Prince House being lit up on all four sides.

"I certainly wasn't about to go in there," Rick explained. "I noted the incident in the log book and went back home."

The next morning, Prince House was thoroughly checked and nothing out of the ordinary was found.

The third floor of Prince House has been sealed off for years. So, why do lights still come on there?

31: Replica Is Also Haunted

Calgary's Heritage Park is a living museum, so it really isn't surprising that so many of its buildings are haunted. Sandstone House, however, is somewhat of a puzzle.

Park employee Diane Schroeder explained that the house is a reconstruction, not an original dwelling. "It was built with materials from other houses, to replicate a sandstone house of that era."

Despite its lack of "intact history" the charming bungalow is haunted. Rocking chairs rock while there's no one sitting in them, and visitors frequently comment to the park interpreters that there's a lady in one of the bedrooms changing a baby's diaper. The first few times they heard this, the news was of concern to park staff, and they went immediately to check it out. There was never anyone there.

Now, when the interpreters hear about the lady with the baby, they just nod knowingly. Many of them have even seen her, and the motherly apparition is accepted as being part of the house. It is anyone's guess which of the three original buildings used to construct the Sandstone house was home to the mother and child during their lifetimes.

Nearby, in front of the Ranch House, a park employee was shocked to see a woman crying. He approached her to offer assistance, but as he did, she disappeared before his eyes. Are the sightings connected in any way? No one knows.

Native Ghost Stories

32: Sweat Lodge Endures

Long before Europeans settled in Alberta, people with a firm belief in the supernatural resided here. The following stories found their way to this author, but I'd be surprised if there weren't many more.

In 1969, the proposed stretch of the Thompson Highway between Rocky Mountain House and Nordegg was surveyed. One of the surveyors discovered a small, native, sweat lodge hidden in the long summer grass. It had been well built. The stone walls were standing and only the willow branches that had been the roof lay broken and weathered, inside the sweat lodge. Under the branches was a small pile of rocks that may have been the stones that had been heated to make the steam.

The surveyor knew the structure would be destroyed during road construction, but he noted it on his drawings anyway. The next year, road building equipment moved in and the sweat lodge was (apparently) demolished.

In the summer of 1971, a group of university students came to re-survey the highway. One of the students noticed the notes about the abandoned sweat lodge on the original map. When they reached that area of the highway, the student went to see if there was anything left.

These remnants may not be haunted but, apparently, there is a sweat lodge that moves of its own accord.

His hunt was rewarded. Hidden in the long summer grasses he found a sweat lodge. It had been carefully built with strong stone walls. The willow roof lay broken inside, burying a small pile of stones.

33: Tales Ensure Protection?

The Alberta badlands are, perhaps, the most dramatic stretch of geography in the province. Among the features in the badlands are hoodoos, which are pillars of rock or clay, caused by erosion and often having strange shapes. It's no wonder the aboriginal people thought the area was very special. Their lore contains many legends; this one is about evil ghosts.

It is said that anyone who ventures out around the hoodoos after dark risks being hit by the dangerous arrows of the long dead, who are called the "night people." These arrows can cause death, disease or disfigurement.

These night people may or may not strike, so the natives never knew whether or not it was safe. To protect themselves, the tribes would perform the ghost dance and offer gifts to the spirits, whenever they had to go near the hoodoos after dark. Today, of course, this ritual is no longer maintained. But the interpreters at Dinosaur Park always re-tell the legend when they talk to visitors about the area and its oddities.

34: Tracks Lead Nowhere

Years before European settlers arrived, the land that is now Waterton National Park was sacred to the natives. It is a windy area, and the aboriginal residents thought that when the wind died down, the Great Spirit walked the land.

One winter, a hunting party of young warriors was caught in an unexpected storm. They sought refuge in the large evergreens that grew on the slopes of the mountains surrounding Waterton Lake. It was nine days before the storm abated and, by that time, all but two of the native hunters had died.

When it seemed safe, the survivors left the sheltering trees and walked along the shoreline toward their village. They hadn't gone far when wind and snow began again. This time the men hid in a small cave in the side of the mountain. Their food had run out and the supply of wood for fires was dangerously low.

When the younger of the two warriors became ill, the older one realized they would both die unless he took action. He fashioned a pair of snowshoes as best he could from the remaining wood and buckskin cut from their clothing. Carrying his sick companion, the warrior headed out across the lake. He hoped the frozen lake would hold their combined weight.

Not long after he started out, the snow stopped falling and the winds died. Everything became very still and cold. The warrior knew the Great Spirit was walking with him. Despite this, the man's strength was completely drained and he knew he would not make it back to the village. The warrior continued as best he was able, his friend over his shoulder, singing praises to the Spirit who was at his side.

The storm ended and a group from the village began a search for their missing warriors. They found those who had died on the mountain slope. After a careful search, they found the prints of snowshoes leading to the middle of the lake. The winds were filling the tracks with freshly fallen snow, but the group was able to follow the path. Without warning the tracks ended. There was no hole in the ice nor any bodies at the end of the snowshoe tracks. The imprints they'd been following simply stopped. The mystery of what became of their fellow villagers was never solved. The two who had survived the first days of the vicious storm had disappeared.

It is said that after an early storm in November, if the winds die down and you know where to look, you can see the tracks of the snowshoes heading across the lake and hear the soft sound of chanting, as though a warrior were praising the Great Spirit.

35: Chief Lives On
In College Plaza

Several years ago, Dr. Bill Meilen, a professor of drama at the University of Alberta, lived in an apartment at College Plaza. The location, across the street from the campus, was ideal for him. He was a busy man with his acting and teaching, so the time saved by not having far to go to work was greatly appreciated.

Despite this apparently ideal site, Dr. Meilen did not live there for long. After playing a particularly challenging roll one evening, Meilen, exhausted, returned to his home, hoping to go directly to bed. Unfortunately, he didn't find the comfort he'd been hoping for. On his way through the halls of College Plaza, Dr. Meilen was stopped by an Indian brave.

"You should not be here," the braided apparition told Meilen. "This ground is sacred. My father was a brave warrior and he is buried here."

And then he was gone, leaving the tired Dr. Meilen badly shaken and unable to fall into the sleep he'd so looked forward to.

36: Leader Rides Again

Chief White Eagle of the Stony tribe led his people, away from attacks, to the safety of what is, today, the Morley area of Alberta. In his lifetime, he was gratified to see that his choice of location was a wise one. His people prospered in the area he'd led them to. Still, the defeat of his people by their enemies, the Cree and the Blackfoot tribes, was a humiliation White Eagle could never accept. He wanted revenge.

Oddly, in death, White Eagle found his satisfaction and retaliation. Mortally injured in a further attack, the brave chief ordered his warriors to bury him at the peak of a nearby mountain. As the younger men prepared the grave for their dying leader, they caused an avalanche of stones to cascade down the mountainside and kill the attacking tribes.

The revenge was so sweet to White Eagle that, even today, he revels in his coup. Legend has it that White Eagle, dressed in flowing robes, rides his white stallion, accompanied by his white dog, through the mists of the Ghost Hills mountains, and then disappears until the next season into the side of Devil's Head Mountain.

37: Chief Makes Good
His Threat

People's fascination with ghosts and ghost stories became very apparent while I was researching this book. News media sometimes went to great lengths to get in touch with me. In tracking me down, a magazine publisher's first call was to the Alberta Government! From there, and within a few days of starting his search, the publisher had been given my number and we had discussed the story he was interested in. (If I'm ever looking for a diligent and resourceful researcher he'll be number one on my list.)

Another determined and successful group were the staff of the "Home Stretch" radio show in Calgary. It's CBC's drive-home program, and they'd been running a series of local ghost stories, interspersed with music and traffic reports!

Bev Oberg from the "Home Stretch" show called me at noon one day. Her problem was rather an immediate one. They had scheduled an interview with an individual who had had an encounter with a ghost. Just hours from air time, the person changed his mind, afraid that his voice would be recognized and that he would be made fun of. Now Bev had empty air-space to fill. Could I be of help?

I may have had more flattering invitations, but the story they wanted me to talk about is one of my favourites — the Deane House. Besides, I could certainly sympathize with their dilemma. Several times, when I'd been following up on potentially exciting ghost stories, people had backed down on their original plan of sharing their stories with me. I could readily empathize with the feeling of frustration.

Bev gave me a couple of hours to get ready and then called me back. I did the interview with the show's host, Jeff Collins, by phone early that afternoon, for broadcast at the appropriate time slot. All went well. Actually, all went better than well because, while I was being interviewed, Jeff gave me a piece of information that helped to solve one of the riddles in the Deane House story. (See Chapter 21.)

I told him about the guest being confronted by the old Indian in the basement during one of the murder mystery night's held at the Deane House.

"I can tell you who that was," Jeff asserted and then continued. "That was Deerfoot. He was a powerful Indian Chief in the Calgary area. Before he died, he warned that he would wreak death and destruction on white men in retaliation for their treatment of his people. Can you imagine that after a threat like that, the city named a high-speed roadway after the chief? That road has had more than its share of personal injury and fatality accidents."

If you have ever driven on Calgary's Deerfoot Trail, you may well be as suspicious as I am that the ghost of Chief Deerfoot has made good his threat.

Other Alberta Ghost Stories

38: Ellen Hopkins
Tells a Story

The original edition of this classic haunted-house yarn is a handwritten document. A teenage girl artistically scripted the pages that begin with a letter written on Christmas Eve 1945 and addressed to the Alberta Folklore Quarterly. *To change even a word of the young woman's manuscript would lessen its value. It is recorded here exactly as Ellen Hopkins wrote it.*

R.R.1 Stony Plain
Dec. 24/45

Alberta Folklore Quarterly
University of Alberta

Gentlemen,

I have written here a story which has been told and retold by my late grandparents and my uncles who staunchly declared every word of it to be the truth. I hope you will consider it suitable for publication and if you do would you send me a copy of the issue of your paper it is in? I am a Grade X Correspondence Student.

Sincerely,
(Miss) Ellen Hopkins, 15 years of age.

I n 1890 my grandfather Lewis Ervin and his bride of one year with their tiny daughter Ellen decided that times were too hard and chances of making a living too slim to remain in their childhood home of Mount Pleasant, Michigan, U.S.A. Having heard wonderful tales of free land and chickens running wild for the taking in midwestern Alberta, they packed their belongings along with great grandmother and grandfather Archer, Uncles Zeke and Jonah and their household effects and moved to what is now the city of Edmonton. At that time it consisted of one frame house, a cottage overlooking what is now the Mount Pleasant Cemetery and several other places of business and smaller private homes.

In south Edmonton there was only a ford crossing of the river below the old Low Level Bridge. The aforementioned frame house was considered quite a luxurious dwelling in that district at that time but alas, for some strange reason there was no one living in it nor had there been for some time.

On a chill November day the Ervins and Archers arrived into the little settlement in search of a house in which to rest their travel weary bones. The gentlemen of the party left the ladies in charge of the baggage while they set off to find said dwelling. The first gentleman questioned informed them that there was a dandy frame house empty for anyone's use who cared to move in and best of all, no rent was required. Upon questioning the good man farther, the ancestors found that a man had lived in it some time ago with his flighty wife. This man had been ill and every night his wife would go out to meet a lover and leave him walking the floor and moaning piteously in his agony until she returned. Then suddenly one day the wife packed in a hurry and left, saying only that her husband had died and was buried on the hill. Soon after a family had moved into the vacant house and moved out after a brief stay of two days, saying that the house was haunted! Grandfather scoffed at the tale and, though the rest of the family were rather sceptical, had them moved in before they knew it.

The first night the travellers slept well and the next day much time was spend in scoffing at superstitious neighbours and their grandmother's tales. But alas, the following night at 12:00 sharp thud thump! thud thump! across the attic floor. It was a windy evening and eerie moans were heard interspersed by clanking as of chains being drawn across a floor! Thud Thump, eee! clank! clank! The spirit was abroad.

Grandmother shot bolt upright in bed and clawed the air wildly her elbow winding up in Grandpa's solar plexus which aroused him out of a deep sleep and set him gasping for air. Sure, and what is it that ye be knockin' me brea..... thud thump clank, eee! Grandpa slid like an eel into the feather tick, burrowing in it up to his ears. Wh-wh-what was that? Grandmother was too frightened to answer and the rest of the night was spent in listening to the noises overhead until the wind went down and the sun arose in all its glory.

That morning a group of white faced Irish Americans after exchanging "did you hear its?" hit upon a plan. That afternoon Grampa took a bag of flour and went upstairs. He sprinkled the flour on the floor and left feeling quite smug. That night the wind came up again howling about the loose shutters and tearing through the barren branches of the big trees behind the little cottage on Mount Pleasant. And soon to the waiting ears of the settlers again came the weird sounds as of a man in agony dragging chains across the upper floor and moaning in agony all the while. This continued until 3:00 and suddenly to the already terrified listeners, although I fancy Grampa's Irish blue eyes were twinkling with fun, came sounds of the piano in the parlour being played!

Uncle Zeke could almost see the ghostly fingers trailing up and down the keys. Thump! the music stopped. Another morning rolled around and it was with some difficulty that grandfather persuaded the family to stay but another day.

That evening the men were returning from town when Uncle Jonah happened to turn and look back down the hill. Rolling up the hill toward them were three balls of fire glowing vividly in the dark. That was enough! Jonah threw up his hands and told his brothers, "Boys, 'tis a warnin' sure and I'm sure of it".

The next morning the frame house was again vacant but not for long. An English family by the name of Bisset moved in at noon and at night they moved out, after summoning Lewis Ervin to board up the windows. This he did and as they were about to leave he asked Mrs. Bisset why they were leaving so soon. For answer she took him inside the house and opened the cellar door. From out of the cellar came an unholy stench. Grandpa Ervin was never a superstitious man but for some reason that smell made the hair raise straight up on his scalp.

No one ever lived in that house again but perhaps the restless spirit. Grandpa never would believe the rest when they tried to tell him t'was a ghost had done all the mischief. He always said that when he went to board up the windows he found a loose shutter which, when banged against the house in the wind, made the thumping noises, for the flour on the floor was undisturbed. The wind howling in an empty bottle made the eerie moaning and it was also the wind rattling the harness in the shed making the clanking noise. The piano had been "played" by a tom cat running over the keys several times and leaping to the floor with a thump.

Several years later he heard some stories of phosphorescent wood glowing in the dark and thought it might well have been that rolled up the hill by the wind which had frightened them. But as for the smell from the cellar it may have been a skunk but, well somehow even Grandpa doesn't think so. So it is possible that this is where Mount Pleasant Cemetery got its name and my ancestors got a huge scare and somehow I think a lot of fun.

By Ellen Hopkins
File No. 7029/45
R.R. 1 Stony Plain, Alberta

This story is reprinted with thanks to its copyright holder, The Alberta Folklore and Local History Collection, Bruce Peel Special Collection Library, University of Alberta.

Unfortunately, there's no record as to whether Ellen Hopkins's story ever made it to publication nearly 50 years ago; however, if she was not a published writer she certainly was an organized one.

The inclusion of a file number under the young lady's signature is also interesting. Were there 7,028 other stories?

39: Hotel Hosts the Famous and the Dead

So many ghost stories surround the Banff Springs Hotel that it is difficult to know where to begin. Perhaps this is why the hotel's Public Relations Department have now decided that, officially, the place is not haunted. A few years ago, the staff spoke openly to the media of many strange and unearthly tales. Fortunately for ghost hunters, these were carefully documented at the time.

The building was originally constructed in 1888, but even the Canadian Pacific Railway's far-sighted William Van Horne had not been able to predict the enormous popularity of the resort. By the early 1900s, several wings had been added to the hotel to keep up with the demand for accommodation. During construction of one of these wings, an error was made. A room with neither doors nor windows was included in the addition. Hastily, the architects altered the blueprints to cover their error. It was not discovered until a fire in the hotel in 1926.

T he secret room was noted during the cleaning-up process, after the fire. What was more intriguing than the room itself, though, was its location. The hallway outside the boarded-up room had been the scene of many reported strange goings-on. Security guards had frequently noted a shadowy figure lurking in the area.

Perhaps the architect who had made the mistake was so haunted by his error in life that he returned to haunt the hotel in death. The missing room was removed during the renovations necessary to repair the fire damage, and that particular ghost has not been seen since.

The most accepted ghost at the Banff Springs Hotel is that of Samuel McCauley. Sam was a Scotsman who arrived at the resort in the 1930s to work as a porter. He stayed on for over forty years, and some say he's there still. Sam, himself, assured anyone and everyone that in death he would return to haunt the hotel.

Guests regularly mention seeing lights shining just outside their windows. The rooms these reports originate from are well above ground level and are located where there are no ledges for anyone to stand on.

One couple checked in late in the evening, and the next day they inquired as to who the old man was who had helped them with their bags the night before. The hotel employee assured them there were no bellhops over the age of thirty at the Banff Springs, but the couple were insistent. They even described the man. They were describing Sam McCauley. He had been dead for two years by that time.

Sam's favourite "haunt" is the ninth floor of the castle-like structure. Legend has it that Sam hid a goodly percentage of his tips up there and that he's come back to protect his money. Whatever his reasons may be, the former employee has certainly kept his word about haunting the hotel.

If Sam ever gets lonely at the Banff Springs, he just needs to visit the resort's Rob Roy Lounge. Here, numerous ghosts have been sighted over the years. These include the ghost of a bride who died after a fall down the hotel staircase, a headless bagpiper, and a long-deceased bartender who takes it upon himself to inform patrons when they've had enough to drink.

Those are the apparitions that have been seen in the lounge. Others exist but have only been heard. These include a male voice that is heard singing in the ladies' washroom at the unlikely hour of 3:00 a.m., and a male chorus that is sometimes heard in the men's washroom.

The MacKenzie Room is another area of the hotel credited with having a ghost. There is a picture of the room's namesake hanging on the wall, and it's said his "spirit comes out of the eyes of the portrait." The ghost is widely believed to be linked to the 1946 fire in the north wing of the hotel.

Most of the guests at the Banff Springs Hotel enjoy the ghost stories that come along with their beautiful surroundings. There is one young man, though, who will probably never return. The Minnesota North Stars hockey team stayed a night in the inn. All the players had heard the ghost stories but, of course, were far too macho to be frightened. All except one rookie that is. His roommate for the night hid under the rookie's bed and, as the young man dropped off to sleep, reached up and grabbed his leg. The older player got the reaction he wanted and laughed as he listened to his teammate screaming down the hallway.

What would the rookie have done if an elderly porter had approached him to ask what was the matter?

40: Skiers' Ghosts

On March 11, 1956, while an avid skier, Charlie Dupre, took his last run down Marmot Peak, an avalanche claimed his life. Today, more than thirty years later, Charlie is still very much a presence on the Marmot Basin ski slopes.

I n 1964, a ski run was named after Charlie, and from that day on, the young Jasper resident has been back on the slopes. According to Art Mulhern, head of security for the resort, the spirit is a playful one who can occasionally carry things a little too far for other employees' liking.

A young man making snow at 2:00 a.m. was surprised to hear the office phone ring. The switchboard was closed, and so the puzzled worker left his post to answer the call. There was "no one" there, and when he returned to his snow-making machine, it had been turned around. Charlie has been credited with the prank because it's typical of the ghostly stunts he's pulled over the years.

You'd think that if an avid skier in life returned to a ski hill, it would be to take advantage of conditions. Charlie Dupre must have had his fill of the slopes because most of his tricks take place inside buildings. Doors mysteriously open and close, dinnerware will be found spread over a floor, and bottles left standing on a shelf have dropped to the floor but remained in an upright position.

The ghost of Charlie Dupre is not a shy one. His pranks have been witnessed by most of the staff at Marmot Basin. Brian Rode, marketing manager for the resort, was quoted recently in the *Edmonton Journal* as saying, "Everyone who has worked around the hill knows of Charlie Dupre's ghost. Any security person who has ever worked at the mid-mountain overnight tells stories of strange happenings such as footsteps in the middle of the night."

This story and the following one lend credence to the theory that even death cannot end a passionate skiers love of the slopes.

*   *   *

In the 1930s, four avid skiers made their way from the United States to the slopes near Lake Louise. They stayed at the Skoki Ski Lodge near the hill and set out to challenge themselves to the limit. The ski patrols repeatedly warned the group not to venture out on their own. There was a great risk of an avalanche and, without an experienced guide, their safety could be in jeopardy.

Since common sense has nothing to do with intelligence – one of the four daring skiers was Christopher Paley, a renowned mathematician – Paley and his three friends set out against the best advice of those who knew the area and its dangers. As was foretold, an avalanche occurred in the Ptarmigan Valley, and the Americans lost their lives.

Poet John Porter recounts their plight in his poem "The Legend of the Halfway House" in which he imagines that upon reaching heaven, the four declined St. Peter's invitation to enter, assuming heaven's ski slopes inadequate for their skills. Porter has them returning to the Lake Louise area to ski into eternity.

Artistic interpretation aside, visitors to the area report seeing lights on and hearing noises coming from an abandoned cabin. The four have also been spotted skiing through the trees. It's not hard to tell the ghostly skiers from the live ones. The four Americans are said to be skiing on fluorescent skis with vermilion flames trailing them.

Perhaps there really is heaven on earth.

41: Resort Builder
Stays On

During William Hayhurst's life, he held a variety of positions: teacher, administrator, politician, store owner and, finally, a resort builder. Since his death, Hayhurst has settled down and is now content to be the ghost of the Sunwapta Falls Bungalows.

The resort is located just outside Jasper and was built by Hayhurst in the early 1940s. Construction was difficult. The war was on and both material and labour were in short supply. Despite these obstacles, the lodge opened in the summer of 1941 and has been running successfully ever since. Perhaps part of the credit for the success should remain with its originator.

Staff at the Bungalows take Hayhurst's presence as an accepted fact. They see him regularly and, even more frequently, feel his presence. Because of this acceptance, they weren't surprised when a couple who had been driving by on the highway arrived at the bungalows quite distraught. It seems the two had spotted a hitchhiker. They had seen him clearly. He was a white-haired man. The couple explained that when they pulled over to let the elderly man into their car, he had vanished. The couple were understandably concerned. The staff, however, weren't surprised at all. The description of the hitchhiker exactly fit that of William Hayhurst.

There's snow in them thar hills. Evidently, there's also the spirits of former residents.

The first years of operation were difficult for Hayhurst and his Sunwapta Falls Bungalows. The resort has changed hands several times since, but Hayhurst's presence has been consistent. His spirit has never threatened anyone, and it's believed that he's just overseeing the business he started over fifty years ago.

42: Arsonist Brazenly Stares From Photograph

Chateau Lake Louise is a sister hotel to the Banff Springs Hotel. Sibling rivalry dictates that this beautiful old building should also hold bragging rights to a ghost. On one wall of the Chateau Lake Louise there hangs a rare photograph – rare, because it includes the image of a ghost. It was taken during the fire of 1924 that all but destroyed the hotel. It was the second time the hotel had been threatened by fire.

The photo shows the fire raging in the background and onlookers in the foreground. Clearly depicted on the back on one of the onlookers' heads, is a face. The hotel staff of that time maintained it was an image of a ghost they knew to be resident in the hotel. It was generally accepted that it was that ghost who had started the fire and that he'd brazenly stayed to watch it burn and even included himself in the photographs being taken of the catastrophe he'd caused.

43: Some People More
Haunted Than Others

Gail's story certainly adds weight to the theory that it is people, not places, that are haunted. She has asked only to be identified by her first name.

T he year was 1977. Gail and her husband headed out of town for a much needed and long overdue vacation. They had planned and looked forward to this time away. It was to be one of those breaks from routine that would be remembered for a lifetime.

"I just couldn't relax, even as we were starting out," Gail began. "I had such an uneasy feeling that there was something wrong."

Gail's tension soon affected her husband's mood as well. Hoping that the feelings would diminish as they drove, the young couple continued to head for their intended destination. Distance from home did nothing to lessen the all-pervasive feelings of doom. They persevered, but two weeks later returned from the disappointing trip feeling worse than when they left.

"On the way back, we stopped and called my husband's family. It was then that we learned that his cousin, who was also our very close friend, had been killed in a car accident the day after we left," Gail recalled, the emotion still evident in her voice even after all these years.

Knowing how desperately the two had needed their vacation, Gail's in-laws had not contacted them about the tragedy. They felt the bad news could wait until the couple's return. The well-meaning family did not take into account Gail's extreme sensitivity.

"As soon as I heard, I knew that it was Chris's death that had caused my feelings. We were so fond of him. He was just a young man. I felt deprived of the chance to say goodbye to him. I cried for a month."

Gail paused to compose herself before continuing. "In bed one evening I felt someone staring at me. I didn't see or hear him, but I knew it was Chris. It was as if he was saying, 'Don't be so sad. I'm happy where I am'."

As a recently deceased person's visit often does, Chris's words were re-assuring to Gail. After his "appearance," she was finally able to get on with her life. Chris, however, apparently continued to keep a special watch over Gail.

"A couple of years later, a young man who had known Chris moved to the city. Steve began coming around and phoning frequently. Neither my husband nor myself were comfortable with him. There was just some-thing about the fellow that we didn't like. One Saturday afternoon the phone rang. When I picked it up the line was full of static. I kept saying hello and asking if there was anyone there, but all I could hear was static. As I started to put the receiver down, the disconnect button began going up and down."

Fascinated, the woman watched until the button finally remained still. She could hardly believe her eyes.

"Do it again," she ordered the unseen force. It did. When the button stopped moving for a second time, Gail's kitchen cupboard doors began to open and close with a will of their own.

"A few minutes later there was a knock at the door. It was Steve. I'm con-vinced to this day that it was Chris who had caused all that strange activity. He was trying to warn me. I didn't let Steve in that day nor have I ever since. As a matter of fact, it's been years since we've even heard from him."

That may not have been the last time Chris visited Gail. In 1979 there was another incident which she suspects was Chris's presence.

"Again, I felt someone watching me. I looked up and in the corner of the living room there was a glowing white light. It was straight up and down. As I stared at it, I felt wonderfully reassured. Then it was gone as quickly as it had appeared."

It may well have been Chris's vigilance that kept Gail from a serious car accident. She was driving home late one night after visiting with her father. The route she took included the stretch of Groat Road in Edmonton leading to the river valley area. The road twists and turns as it makes it's way down the hill.

It was very late and there was little traffic. In keeping with a long standing habit, Gail was driving in the left lane.

"Something was telling me to change lanes, to get into the right lane. The feeling was so strong that I couldn't ignore it. As soon as I did, I rounded another curve and there in the left lane was an abandoned car, with no lights on. It was just sitting there. If I hadn't changed lanes, I would have crashed into it, full force."

With some justification, Gail wonders if it was Chris's spirit guarding her.

Later that same year Gail had another experience. This one definitely did not involve Chris. Gail readily admitted the incident: "It scared hell out of me."

She awakened in the middle of the night from a deep sleep.

"My first waking thought was that a cat was crawling up the bed. Then I felt as though something was trying to take over my body. I cried out, 'God help me' and instantly I was surrounded by a white light."

Unable to get back to sleep, Gail wandered aimlessly through the apartment until morning. Shortly after day-break, a neighbour came to report that there had been a suicide in the building the night before. It had happened at the time of Gail's terrifying experience.

"As soon as I heard about the man's death, I knew what had caused my terror. In retrospect I'm sure that he didn't really want to kill himself. He'd changed his mind, but it was too late."

It was months before Gail recuperated from her experience. Since these incidents, the couple has moved. As they were settling into their new place, her husband wondered out loud if the spirits would follow them. Just a few days later, as Gail was sitting at her kitchen table reading, his question was answered.

"The table began to move as though someone were shaking it. My son and I both watched it happen."

When the violent movement stopped, Gail and the boy stared at each other in disbelief.

"Do it again," she commanded the table, as she had done to the phone. The table began to move of its own accord once more.

"I guess that answered our question," Gail conceded.

44: Strange Stories from Camrose

Touring the province and stopping to chat has proved to be a rewarding way to turn up strange tales. While enjoying the beautiful area around Camrose, a county worker added the following two stories to the collection.

In 1910 a wealthy Englishman arrived in the Camrose area. He was newly married and intended to settle in this picturesque Alberta community. Because his bride was used to the best, he built a big two-storey home in preparation for her arrival. When it was complete, he sent for her and the young woman made her way by ship and train to her husband's side.

The bride's reaction to her new home was swift and sure. She hated everything about it and refused to even spend a night in the home her husband had laboured to build. Devastated, the man returned to England with his wife. He left the house just as it stood. No information was left about when he'd return or what he wanted to do with the residence.

Years passed and the house stood empty. No one ever heard from the Englishman again. His house, however, began to take on a life of its own. Neighbours observed lights going on and off in the bedroom windows.

Soon, the whole town accepted the eccentric English couple's abandoned home as being haunted. It was presumed that by now the man had died and had come, in death, to live where he'd intended to, years before.

The house was eventually claimed for unpaid taxes. Despite this, it wasn't torn down, and the activity in the windows of the always empty house continued. It wasn't until the early 1980s that the lot and house were purchased by a developer. By the time the once-stately and imposing residence was torn down, it was sadly dilapidated; it had never served it's original purpose. Maybe.

*   *   *

The second tale from the County of Camrose took place more recently, in the early 1970s. At that time, a couple with six children settled on a farm near Edberg. They were a hardworking family who did not bother much with neighbours or socializing. The children, did, though, attend a local school and were able, here, to have some fun and make some friends.

More than a year after they'd moved to the area, the children's teachers were surprised to find all the brothers and sisters absent from school one day. It was presumed that they were kept home to help with the chores. When none of the children appeared for several days, surprise turned to concern and an official of the school was sent to the family home to investigate.

No one was at home when the official arrived. By peering through windows, he could see that they had not moved but were merely away. All the furniture was still in the house, and the place was scrupulously clean and orderly. There was little anyone could do except wait for the day the family returned from their unexpected holiday.

Nearly twenty years have passed, and that day has not yet come. Not one member of the self-isolated family has ever been seen since. For all intents and purposes, eight people vanished in the 1970s from rural, central Alberta.

That, in itself, is a strange tale, but what makes it stranger still is the house the six children and their parents left behind. Up till the mid-

1980s, the house still existed, abandoned. No one remembers the land being sold or the dwelling being torn down, so it may well still exist. Its exact location has been forgotten by area residents and, today, the place is confused with a number of abandoned farm houses. If you did happen upon it, though, there is one way you'd know for sure you'd found the right homestead.

Despite the years of abandonment, the interior of this house apparently remains immaculate, as clean and tidy as the day the owners left it, with no one seen going in or out.

Some abandoned homesteads like this one are said to be eerily possessed. To this day, no one knows why the residents of one of them disappeared, or where they went.

45: Historic Bed and Breakfast Has Unusual Guest

Lorene Frere of Trochu has resurrected a unique piece of Alberta history, single handedly. Without her dogged determination a distinctive segment of the province's past would have been lost. The story of the St. Ann's Ranch also, happily, includes some ghostly sightings.

Lorene and her husband, Louis, own the ranch. It was their home while they were raising their family of six children, and it has stayed their home. Lorene now operates a quaint tea room and a bed-and-breakfast business, out of the original ranch headquarters.

The building dates back to 1904 when Armand Trochu and his partners Joseph Devilder and Leon Eckenfelder settled on the land and started what was to become the area's pivotal business.

The men were French aristocrats and officers in the cavalry. Deeply religious, Trochu named the ranch St. Ann's in honour of the patron saint of Trochu's birthplace, Brittany, France. That homage is still evident in the carved statue of St. Ann that looks out from above the doorway to the tea room. By coincidence, St. Ann is also Lorene's patron saint.

She explained, "When I joined the church, the priest suggested that, as my middle name is Ann, St. Ann could be my patron saint."

In the early days of the century, the ranch prospered and other adventurers from France joined the industrious pioneers. One of those was Philomene Butruille, Joseph Devilder's sister. She, her husband, five children, a cook, a governess, a maid, and thirty-two pieces of luggage had accompanied Butruille when she emigrated. That must have made quite the convoy as they arrived at the homestead!

Not long after that, Devilder left Canada and returned to France. His sister, Philomene, stayed behind to continue running the store that had been established at the ranch. After the death of her first husband, Philomene married Pappiard, another of the cavalry men. Together, they remodelled and enlarged the ranch house. Today, it looks much as it did in Philomene Butruille's time.

"She must have been quite a woman," Lorene Frere said, with obvious admiration for her home's previous owner. Not many years later, all but two of the French families left the area they'd made their home. World War I had broken out and as these men were members of the cavalry and staunch patriots, they immediately headed back to France to help defend their native land. Of the original settlers, only descendants of the Freres and the de Beaudraps remain in the Trochu area.

"My husband's Grandma and Grandpa never spoke much about the past," Lorene explained. "Even if people came out here to interview her about the significance of the ranch, Grandma didn't say too much. She just took the story of the ranch and the town's settlement in her stride. It was their life, so I guess they didn't think of it as being very exciting."

Lorene and Louis had been living at the ranch and raising their children there, when Lorene was approached by the committee doing the local history book.

"They thought that as I lived on the land where it all began, I might want to research the history of the coulee. I was quite busy with family life, but I did spend as much time as I could in museums and archives. I'd never done anything like that before and I just loved it."

Considering the original nature of the investigations, it's apparent Lorene Frere was a natural researcher. However, family demands at the time were such that she wasn't able to pursue the investigation past what was needed for the local history project.

The original part of this home on St. Ann's Ranch in Trochu was built by French settlers in 1904.

"When my children were grown and I was faced with empty nest syndrome, I remembered how much I enjoyed all those hours spent digging into the history of our home."

She brought the box of research material down from the attic where it had been stored for several years and started again in earnest. It wasn't long before Lorene realized that they were living in a piece of history.

In 1989 the St. Ann Ranch was designated a provincial historic site, and that year, in July, Lorene Frere opened part of the thirty-room building as a seasonal tea room and a year-round bed and breakfast. This seems a very ambitious undertaking for someone who has never had any experience in the hospitality industry. Although Lorene exudes a quiet confidence, this project was potentially strewn with pitfalls. Amazingly, there was never a problem.

"Everything went so smoothly when we were working towards the opening. It seemed that whatever I'd need next would be there for the taking. If I decided on a particular fabric to decorate with, I'd find it and it would be on sale. If I needed an extension cord to continue working, I'd just walk around the corner and find one just the length I needed. It was amazing."

It was during this time that Lorene found a prayer book to St. Ann in the attic of the ranch. She began doing a daily devotion centred around passages in the sacred book. As St. Ann is both her personal patron saint and that of her beloved home, she wondered if all her good fortune wasn't divinely inspired. Not surprisingly, the devout lady has kept up this tradition.

Perhaps this is why, when listening to Lorene talk about her labour of love and its historical significance, you can hear the respect she has for those early God-fearing French settlers. The impression she gives is that of a guardian of a sacred trust. As a result, the atmosphere is so warm and inviting that even guests who are travelling on business report that they are immediately relaxed.

All of this makes a strange and contradictory background for a ghost story, but perhaps that is fitting, too. St. Ann's Ranch is not ordinary, either from an historical or present-day perspective. In the twenty-one years the Freres have called the building home, no member of the family has ever reported any unusual sightings, noises or occurrences. Considering the colourful background, this is surprising but true.

The night before the bed and breakfast opened to receive guests, the town of Trochu was hit with a tremendous hail storm. "Roofers arrived from out of town to repair the damage that had been done to the houses in town," Lorene remembered. "The morning after they arrived, one of the men was quite upset. He asked me if the place was haunted."

Lorene assured the man that she'd lived there a number of years and to her knowledge it wasn't haunted. The man's question certainly made her curious and she inquired as to why he'd ask about such a thing. With little prompting, he told the lady that he'd seen a young woman at the end of his bed. She was trying to say something to him but was having a hard time talking. It was clear the tradesman had been badly shaken by what he'd experienced. Despite the three-night booking the roofers had made, the Freres never saw them again. If they finished their work in town, they stayed somewhere else for the next two nights.

Nothing unusual occurred for a while and the incident was largely forgotten in the excitement of the new and growing business. That is until Lorene invited two friends back to the ranch after a meeting they'd all attended in town.

"I asked the ladies if they'd like to look around while I made the tea," Lorene offered.

One of the women, who has asked to be identified by the pseudonym, Patty, saw or felt more than the other.

"I'm not a psychic," Patty began. "But I do seem to be extremely sensitive. As we approached the set of stairs that leads to the top of the house, I had the strangest sensation. I felt there was a girl or a woman, probably someone in her late teens, standing at the top of the stairs, wearing a blue, calf-length dress. She kept looking out the window toward the southeast. I got the clear impression that she had lived there but that she was waiting for something or someone. It wasn't a scary feeling at all."

She paused before adding an explanation: "I've had these experiences before. The sensation wasn't unpleasant. It was quite liveable. I felt the girl was friendly but lonely."

Patty also received the impression that the young woman had recently had a love affair with a man in a uniform.

"RCMP maybe? I don't know, but I had a clear impression of the two of them under the tree together, in front of the ranch."

Patty was unaware that the North West Mounted Police had been stationed at the ranch or that Philomene's governess had married a man named Tucker, who served as a corporal with the forerunner of today's Mounties. Their wedding was held at the ranch house and Lorene has preserved some photographs she'd discovered of the happy occasion.

"Even though I'd never been in the place before, I knew, too, that a particular doorway led to a storage room. I strongly associated that storage room with a severely handicapped child. I had the impression of the child being wheeled around from room to room."

Her sensations were unnervingly accurate. Louis Frere's cousin had lived out her short life at the ranch. Theresa was the child's name, but her nickname was BooBoo and she was always called that. BooBoo was born normal but became badly damaged by a misplaced intravenous needle. She was blind and mute. Up to the age of three, she could stand for short periods of time. Slowly, BooBoo lost even that ability and she spent her days in a crib that was equipped with castors so that she could be pulled from room to room.

Despite the extensive brain damage, the child's hearing was obviously keen. She loved music, seemed to recognize people by their voices, and would smile at her mother's voice. The child died peacefully at the age of fifteen while living at the ranch.

Patty had no knowledge of any of this and was aghast to learn that the storage room where she'd sensed the child's presence still held the crib that was home to BooBoo.

Discussing it three years later, Patty decided it was time for a return visit to St. Ann's Ranch.

"There's lots there," she stated simply.

More recently, a man travelling on business stayed overnight at the ranch. Before turning in for the night, he asked for an early morning wake-up call. He slept deeply all night and was surprised to wake up to the image of a young woman at the foot of his bed. He thought this was an extremely unusual wake-up call. By the time he was able to fully clear the sleep from his head, the girl had disappeared. His wake-up call came in the standard form of a ringing telephone, not long after.

"You know, he never said a word to me about the experience," Lorene said. "I heard about it through the grapevine."

To date, not one member of the Frere family has felt or seen anything unusual about their enormous home.

46: Phenomenal Castle

Spooky tales of old, haunted castles in the British Isles and Europe are legion. The following story is like one of those, but with a couple of dramatic differences. The castle is located in northern Alberta and it's only thirteen years old. In keeping with tales from abroad, Alberta's castle is filled with ghosts and unexplained phenomena.

Margo Legasse was born and raised in the St. Paul area of the province. As a young woman, she became a teacher and moved east to Montreal to pursue her career. After marrying and having children, Margo decided to return to the area of her hometown.

"Someone owed our family a great deal of money," Margo explained, while seated at a picnic bench in the main room of her castle. "He didn't have any money but he did have concrete blocks. I decided to accept those instead and set about drawing plans for the building I have here."

The year was 1979 and the location Margo chose was completely isolated, roughly fifteen kilometres north of St. Paul on a bluff overlooking St. Vincent Lake.

"It used to be my 'hideaway'. Now, I have neighbours," the lady said, indicating other homes within sight of her beloved grey cinder-block castle.

"The first week we were here I woke up every morning at 3:30 a.m., hearing footsteps walking back and forth across the ceiling. I thought it was my sons and I would go up and knock on their door and tell them to be quiet and go to sleep," Margo explained in her lilting English that is based in Alberta's unique version of French.

"But the boys were asleep and they got mad at me for waking them up like that every night. They hadn't heard anything at all."

After listening to these heavy footsteps for several nights in a row, Margo got up the courage to investigate.

"I climbed up on the roof but there was no one there. I was the only one who was hearing this noise. I didn't sleep until daybreak for weeks. Then finally I swore at him, whoever he was, and told him to stop. That did it. After that it was usually quiet at nights."

The staircase to the second floor of the castle is a circular, metal one. As you climb up or down it, you make two complete 360-degree turns. While her sons and their fellow musicians watched and listened, the staircase shook, one stair at a time, and the heavy footsteps that had routinely been heard on the ceiling proceeded down the stairs.

"Those boys went 'bazookas' I'll tell you. They went to bed and locked the doors to the bedroom. That didn't stop them hearing party noises from the next room. There was laughing and bells but there was no one there."

It's not likely the Legasse boys were ever inconvenienced by other musicians wanting to use the castle for practice sessions.

The circular staircase figured in another sighting Margo explained.

"My son was sitting on the chesterfield, and a woman with blonde hair and wearing a long dress came down the stairs and beckoned to him to come with her. He didn't."

Margo's husband has never lived in the castle, and her sons have since moved away. She doesn't teach any more but sculpts full time.

"I loved teaching but I decided to enjoy life," she said quietly. Tim Landru, a young construction worker in the area, lives in the castle with Margo now and helps her with the upkeep. He, too, has had an experience on the staircase.

"I was walking up the stairs and something grabbed the back of my

A turret on St. Paul's haunted castle is just one of the spooky features of this rural Alberta landmark.

knee. It really scared me and I ran the rest up of the flight," Tim recalled. Then he added, "There's also the thing in the bush."

"Yes," Margo continued. "We have an outdoor privy. Twice when I've been out there, I've heard the sound of a heavy animal, like a moose, running straight at me. It was terrifying. I was sure I was going to be trampled. It's happened to others out there, too, but there's never anything there."

Tim added, "No one's heard that for awhile now. It seems once you stand up to the fear you feel of this noise, you never hear it again. Whatever it is preys on people who are afraid of it."

Why would anyone stay on under such stressful circumstances? Margo answered matter of factly. "I've thought of leaving. I had a realestate agent come out and take a look at the place. When she walked in, it started to rain and you could tell she was very uncomfortable. As she looked out the window, a ball of lightning struck. It hung suspended in the middle of that window for a moment. I told the agent, 'Never mind. I can never leave this place.' Since then, whatever spirits are here seem more settled. Still, before I leave to go away anywhere, I say out loud how much I love this place and that I'd never leave it, and I explain that I'll be back. That seems to help."

That was in 1980, and Margo has kept her word. In return, the atmosphere in the castle has improved.

"When my mother was alive, she refused to come here because there were such dreadful smells. Sometimes it smelled like burning flesh. That smell would get into your hair and it just wouldn't wash out. You couldn't leave a loaf of bread out for more than an hour or it would pick up this horrible smell, too."

It was only through Margo's kindness that the castle was finally ridden of the putrid aroma. She offered the castle to a young priest to use as a retreat.

"After he left I never smelled that foul odour again. When I saw him next, he didn't speak of it directly but he did go to great lengths to tell me of previous exorcisms he'd done."

Although the putrid smell has not returned, the castle is not entirely rid of mysterious smells. Occasionally, either Margo or Tim will experience whiffs of sweet smells that are extremely localized.

"You can just be sitting in the chair reading and suddenly, out of nowhere, smell something very sweet. Or you might be walking from room to room and in one particular spot there'll be a very strong but pleasant smell. Occasionally when I'm baking and I check what's in the oven, I get either a foul or sweet smell that is not what you'd expect from baking. Then the next time I'll check, it'll just smell like baking. Whatever it is likes to be acknowledged. We pay attention to it and then it goes away."

Unfortunately, Margo has discovered this method does not always work.

"A stain appeared on the floor. It smelled terrible. I scrubbed and scrubbed at it, but it just got worse. Finally, I just left it alone and eventually it went away," Margo remembered.

As well, phantom music occasionally pervades the castle.

"People across the bay have heard organ music coming from here. They said it was lovely. There was no one here that night and there's never been an organ in the place. I've heard flute music from nowhere, and once I heard a guitar being played upstairs. It was so real that I ran and got a neighbour. I was sure there was a person up there. The neighbours wouldn't come though. They were afraid it wasn't a person!" Margo chuckled at the memory.

One time, Margo's natural curiosity made her leave the entity a note. She told it, "If you're human, eat." The next day the shade from the little lamp she'd left the note under was broken into tiny, uniform pieces. That, apparently, was the answer. Over the years Margo has come to accept that the building is hers and that she's safe there.

This safety does not always include the right to a full night's sleep, however. Only a few years ago, she was wakened by a figure of a man standing beside her bed.

"He was so clear in my mind that I could draw him," the lady explained in her soft voice. "He had an open shirt and a moustache. He appeared to me a few times, and then I realized I recognized him. I asked him what he wanted. He told me to go to his mother who lives in St. Paul and tell her that he is happy where he is. I didn't want to do that, because I knew the woman and she wasn't very approachable."

After a few more visits from the young, deceased man, Margo overcame her hesitancy. She knocked on the woman's door and before the man's mother could say anything, Margo explained her mission.

"I told her that I must speak and speak quickly or else this will not get said. Then I gave her the message from her son and I went away without another word."

The last time the young man appeared to her, he stood at the head of her bed. He smiled down at the woman and then disappeared into a column of smoke.

Although there have been no further apparitions at the castle, rooms will mysteriously light up with a creamy white glow.

"When that happens, there are no shadows," Margo explained. "And

Tim watched balls of light about the size of softballs bounce all around him while he was working outside."

Margo has investigated the history of the land her castle sits on. So far she really hasn't determined anything significant.

"Locals say maybe the castle sits on an ancient Indian burial ground. I don't see how that would explain it, because when I've seen someone they've been European, not native. I don't know what has caused all this. I do know there is a strong field of energy running through this castle. A physics student found it and demonstrated it to me. If you move your hand in a circle just by the castle door you'll feel it."

Margo Legasse invited me to try the method she'd been told to use to feel the field of energy. I did feel something but suspected it was only nervousness at being in such unusual surroundings. Toward the end of the interview, Margo took me up the circular staircase to try the extension of the field on the second floor. There was no mistaking the strange sensation on the palm of my hand that time. It tingled as though it was "asleep" but it felt very warm, instead of the cold feeling that normally accompanies that sensation.

Something very out of the ordinary is at work in Margo Legasse's rural Alberta castle.

47: Knocking Around
in a Trapper's Cabin

The Fort McMurray area has a turbulent history. Its weather is harsh and the area has been severely affected by Alberta's boom-bust economy, so the faint-hearted don't settle there.

When the economy boomed, little communities sprang up around oilsands plants. These "instant towns" usually adopted a frontier mentality, and life's little "niceties" were neither available nor desired. In the early 1970s, all that remained of one such neighbourhood was an abandoned trapper's cabin.

A native elder from the area reports that at one time the land the cabin sat on was a temporary home to about a hundred people. Apparently they were a violent, hard-drinking group who were known to settle their differences in a very permanent way. "Several" murders were committed while the shanty town was in existence.

On a frigid November evening in 1974, two trappers were relieved to come across an abandoned cabin. They were on a trek to town for supplies and they were going to camp out, but it had turned colder and the shelter was a comforting sight. Even the trappers' dogs would be protected for the night as the cabin was surrounded with small outbuildings.

As soon as they'd settled the dogs, the two went about making themselves at home. It was bitterly cold in the tiny house. Colder, it seemed, than it was outside. They built a fire.

"That should take the frost out of the air in no time," they thought.

Unfortunately, no matter what they did, they could not raise the temperature of the little peaked-roof building. These were not men who were accustomed to luxury, and they dealt with the heating problem in a typically matter-of-fact way. They tucked into their bedrolls and looked forward to a good night's sleep.

No sooner had they put their heads down than they clearly heard the distinctive sound of wood being chopped. Assuming they were very much alone in the area, the sounds were puzzling. The trappers left their beds and headed out to look around. Nothing could be seen or heard despite a thorough search. There were not even any tracks in the snow.

The dogs had been completely silent and this caused the men to blame the sound of chopping on their imaginations. A quick check of the dogs did nothing to reassure the pair that this was a correct assumption. Like their masters, these dogs had not been used to an easy existence and yet they were crouched down and shivering, clearly frightened. No amount of talking to them or patting them offered any relief for their obvious fright.

Deciding there was nothing else they could reasonably do, the trappers returned to the cabin in the hopes of sleeping. As soon as they did, the sounds of chopping could be heard coming from just outside the cabin. Again they went outside and searched and again they could find nothing.

After three or four fruitless searches, it was decided that one would sleep while the other stayed awake watching out for intruders. Every time the trapper appointed to the position of guard would put his head down, the chopping would start up again, and every time he went outside to investigate, it would cease. This pattern continued until the poor man, totally unnerved, collapsed into a fitful but exhausted slumber.

When they awoke in the morning, all was quiet and the dogs were tranquil. Despite the calm, the men had had more than enough of the cabin. Without bothering to fix breakfast, the two men harnessed their dogs and fled toward town. In 1984, the trappers were quoted as saying they would never spend another night in the cabin and that the experience was one they hoped never to encounter again.

48: Settler Loves
His Land

Nineteen hundred and twelve was a dynamic year in the new province of Alberta. Schools were opening, roadways were being constructed, the Legislature Building was completed and immigrants were arriving by the hundreds to settle the vast land.

The Houghtons were among those settlers; they homesteaded on land ten miles southeast of Westlock. Husband and wife worked together to clear the land and build a small house. Not too many years later, they were blessed with two sons, in addition to the son who'd been born before they left the old country.

Fearing their sons would go uneducated if they remained so isolated, the Houghtons moved their family to another homestead, this one only a mile from the school. The move was difficult because the father, especially, loved the land they'd first come to. He had moved away only for his sons' futures. His determination to return to his beloved homestead and build a larger home never wavered. Unfortunately, he was never to realize his dream. Butch Houghton died ten years after his boys started school.

The original little house was moved to the new homestead so the grandmother could be near her widowed daughter. Years later, the middle son took over the old homestead and turned it into a prosperous farm. Despite the fact he never married, the son eventually tore down the original house and built a much larger one. He lives on in the home to this day.

Because of his age, the independent man is not able to get around as well as he once did, so he has had the second storey of his old home sealed off. There is no way to reach the top floor from the inside of the house. The only possible way anyone could gain access to the upper storey is by propping an extension ladder against an outside wall and climbing in a window – certainly not a feat a frail gentleman in his eighties would attempt.

Oddly, since the sealing off was completed, the place has become somewhat of a neighbourhood curiosity. Orange, green and red lights are frequently reported glowing and moving in the second-storey windows.

49: Grandma Watches Writers

Four miles from the village of Pickardville, northwest of Edmonton, two men built a house for their aging mother. The woman had worked hard all her life to make a living for herself and her sons. She had done without over the years and her sons were determined that, at last, she would have the comfortable home she'd dreamed of.

By the time she moved into her dream house, the woman was badly crippled with arthritis and was only able to look at her land, which she did with pride. Shortly after, the woman died. Not wanting to get rid of their mother's possessions, the sons merely moved everything into the attic. One of the sons moved into the house and lived there for the rest of his life. When he died, the old place stood empty until the woman's granddaughter, a writer by profession, decided the house would make an ideal working retreat.

After having the abandoned house cleaned and fixed up, the granddaughter began to use it as the isolated hideaway she needed to do her writing. Right from the start, she felt something unusual in the house, but she put the feeling down to the unaccustomed isolation.

One weekend, she invited a fellow writer to join her. They spent a pleasant afternoon and evening enjoying one another's company and the quiet of the home. In the evening, as they were sitting in the living room discussing writing, the guest looked up and saw the face of an old woman in a doorway. The granddaughter saw the expression on her friend's face and followed her gaze. There was the face of her grandmother. The apparition looked intently at both women, then gave a nod of her head and disappeared. She has never returned. She doesn't have to. Her granddaughter knows, now, that she is welcome and protected in the once-abandoned home in Pickardville.

50: Two Tales from Small Towns

Ghost stories are all supposed to have occurred "many years ago" and in exotic locations. This one, however, took place in April of 1992 in the town of Lamont, Alberta.

A woman drove out to see her mother in Lamont. The two chatted happily for awhile, and the daughter noted how well her mother seemed. The younger woman had some errands, so she left to get these done before she drove back home.

While walking along the street, the daughter saw a man coming toward her. She stood still and stared at the approaching figure in utter shock. It was her father, and he had died years before.

When he came within a few feet of her, he spoke. "I have come to take your mother home," he explained.

That night, the woman's mother fell and was taken to the hospital. After examining the woman, the doctors said she was fine and could go home the next day. The following morning she died from complications caused by the fall.

* * *

Due south of Lamont lies Tofield, Alberta. It is one of a string of small towns along Highway 14 and the railway tracks that run parallel to it. South and east of Edmonton, Tofield is not too far from Viking, hometown of the National Hockey League's Sutter brothers.

This story, like some others, was frustrating to try to nail down. The people involved were no longer willing to talk about their strange experiences by the time they were contacted. The message was relayed to me this way: "I have a hard enough time talking about this to my friends. I'm certainly not going to discuss it with a stranger."

The following story, though, had already been told to me by a young woman I've known for years. She knows the Tofield family and never imagined they'd be unwilling to share their experiences.

T he family in question consists of a husband, wife and two children, who had settled into their newly purchased Tofield home easily. Nothing seemed amiss until the day the husband was sitting in his living room, watching television. A movement in the periphery of his vision distracted him from the show he'd been enjoying.

Looking toward the movement, the man was most startled to see someone in his living room. Worse, this man was not the clean-cut sort who might have been welcome. The uninvited visitor was, judging by his clothes and rather unkempt appearance, a motorcycle gang member. The startled homeowner had a few seconds to assess the half-Wellington boots, blue jeans, helmet and requisite black leather jacket. Then the image was gone. It had walked through a wall and out of sight.

The man jumped up from where he'd been sitting and hurried, via the doorway, to the adjacent room, and then another, and then another, until he'd checked the whole house thoroughly. The "biker" was nowhere to be found. The man was as alone in his house as he had presumed he was. Despite this, his composure was understandably shaken.

Since that first incident many years ago, the "biker" has used the family's home as a route to wherever he had to get on several occasions. Even in life, a motorcycle gang member can prove an intimidating sight. The ghost of one would be even more startling a vision.

For this family, though, that's no longer the case. They're used to his forays through their home. Not only is the ghost not menacing, he seems oblivious to the family's existence. Who says life in small-town Alberta is boring?

51: Priest Watches
Over His Mission

The Lac La Biche Mission occupies the same site it did when originally established in 1855 by the Missionary Oblates. The contributions the mission made to the settlement of the province were significant. It housed the first printing press, the first sawmill, and the first convent, and the mission grew the first commercial wheat crops. The stone foundations from the convent were unearthed by archaeologists in 1990.

In 1920 a tornado swept across the Lac La Biche countryside, flattening buildings for miles around. The church and many other buildings on the mission site were completely destroyed. Amazingly, the church's altar was left untouched and sits, today, in the "new" church, constructed in 1921. Services continue to be conducted from this altar. Past and present congregations regard its very existence as a miracle.

The other buildings on the site today include the "new" convent (built in 1890) and the rectory, which, like the church, was built after the tornado. The mission is a museum, open for the public to enjoy. It is well staffed with well-informed interpreters.

Some of the staff know stories about the place that will never be written up in history books. A young lady who asked to be called Jane is one of those who remember.

"In 1989 three of us were working in and around the rectory. We'd frequently see the reflection of a person in one of the windows. We'd go to check it out and there'd be nothing there. This happened four or five times before we finally got used to it. I never felt worried about it."

Whoever or whatever the reflection belonged to obviously didn't want to bother the young people working or be bothered itself.

"He looked to me to be a sad, old man. He appeared most often on gloomy days that were overcast with clouds."

Could the weather conditions have created the illusions the young people were witness to? Carey McDonald was a tour guide at the mission in 1982. During her tenure, she had experiences that supported Jane's story.

"Oh, yes, I've seen the ghost in the rectory," she confided. "And I've heard about him from others too."

While working at cleaning the grounds behind the rectory, the staff would frequently get the feeling they were being watched. This bothered them because they knew they were the only ones on the property. It wasn't long before they noticed the image of a man standing staring at them from out of a window.

"We went in the building and up to the attic to check it out. There was nothing there, but we'd all seen the same man, a priest. We high-tailed it out of the building."

Once sensitized to the existence of the priestly ghost, Carey and her workmates kept their ears open for others with similar stories. Their attentions were rewarded.

"Actors from the play *North Song* that was put on here also said they'd seen the ghost. Some said they'd seen him watching them as they woke up. One person told me he noticed an open window and went to shut it. When he looked back, the window was open again and a priest was sitting by it, reading a newspaper."

When a mission reunion was held, Carey's experiences were further confirmed.

"Former students were full of ghost stories. The priest was a consistent

In 1920, a tornado destroyed the original Lac La Biche Mission church, except for the altar. This and a nearly human presence occupy the current buildings.

figure throughout them all. A couple who were staying at the convent during the reunion reported that they could get close to each other but could not touch."

Can the energy of chastity remain in a building?

"I've always really liked the convent, although I did see an image in a third-floor window there one time," Carey remembered. People frequently asked Carey how she could even go into the buildings after so many frightening reports and experiences.

"Each one of us sort of 'adopted' a room and took special care of that particular area. I think that the spirits knew we weren't doing any harm and that we were fixing the place up."

She continued describing how she felt protected by what she and her peers had been doing. "I've scrubbed every inch of the walls in the drawing room," she said, and then added with a lilt in her voice, "Sure, it's eerie, even to this day, but it's also fun comparing stories with all the others."

52: Stories from
a Folklore Collection

The following ghost stories were all recorded in 1945. It's not known when the incidents occurred. By now, the people who had the extraordinary experiences might well be spirits themselves.

Gus Erickson has an interesting lot of ghost stories to tell. His best concerns a haunted house. One night, while looking over his trap line, he was caught out in a storm. Fortunately he found an abandoned log cabin, and he was glad to take shelter in it, and make his bed upon the floor. About midnight he was wakened by somebody passing a hand over his face. He sat up and lit a match. Nobody was in the room. He lay back and went to sleep. Soon he was wakened by the hand again. Again he lit a match and found nothing. This time when he lay down he did not go to sleep. He was convinced that something or somebody was playing tricks on him, and was determined to catch the phoney spook. As soon as he had quieted down, the hand passed over his face once more. Instantly his own hand flashed out – and he encountered nothing at all.

Later he investigated the history of that old shack, and he found that it had once been the home of an old woman living alone. The old lady had long since moved away, but shortly before he spent the night in that old building, she had died. Gus says he wouldn't have felt so comfortable if he had suspected that the woman was his visitor that night.

* * *

One winter night as Gus Erickson was walking home, he heard the jingling of sleigh bells, and turned to discover a team of black horses drawing a cutter, trotting down the road behind him. Thinking to catch a ride home, he stopped in the middle of the road and waited. But the team went as far as a neighbour's corner and turned into the yard. It went past the house, past the barn, and went jingling off through the woods.

"That's queer," thought Gus. "There's no road out that way."

And so he went back to the corner to investigate. But he found no tracks!

* * *

Mrs. John Szapko tells a ghost story which happened more recently. (Editor's note: "more recently" would refer to the year 1945). One morning she awoke early and found her father standing in the bedroom. She was terribly frightened, for she knew that her father was in far-away Germany.

"Are you all right, Hedy?" the old man asked.

"Yes, father," she replied.

"Then snuggle a little closer to Johnny."

Laughing heartily, the old fellow turned and stamped out of the house.

John was wakened by his wife's quivering, and asked what the trouble was.

"My father was here a few minutes ago," she said.

However, that very day Mrs. Szapko received a cable stating that her father had just died.

These stories are reprinted with the kind permission of the Alberta Folklore and Local History Collection, Bruce Peel Special Collection Library, University of Alberta.

53: "An Area of Concentrated Suffering"

"There is little point in denying it," Monica Field of the Frank Slide Interpretive Centre commented when asked if the area is haunted. "This is an area of such concentrated suffering. The only place I've ever been that I felt that suffering as intensely was the Tower of London."

The Crowsnest Pass area was coal-mining country in Alberta's early days. Hard living and inadequate safety precautions snuffed out a number of lives prematurely, but mass tragedy was the result of the worst and most dramatic events. Three tiny towns were devastated between the years 1903 and 1914.

On April 29, 1903, while most of the town of Frank slept, almost an entire side of nearby Turtle Mountain crashed down. The avalanche is estimated to have taken only a minute and a half. It killed at least 76 people. Very few bodies were ever recovered, and the lethal rocks remain where they fell, forming a mass headstone.

There has never been any attempt to remove the detritus. Today an interpretive centre details the tragedy and explains that the strange geography and geology surrounding the area are monuments to the destructive power of nature. The death toll may have been far higher than the recorded figure. An accurate count will never be possible because all the town records were buried with the bodies, and the "boom town" of Frank had a constantly shifting population.

Turtle mountain stays on, but this rocky terrain and the groans of victims are the legacy of the 1903 Frank Slide.

Fifty men had apparently arrived in Frank the day before. It isn't known whether they'd continued on to the neighbouring town of Blairmore or if they were killed by the slide as they lay in makeshift tents.

The details that are known are perhaps even more surprising. In Frank Anderson's book about the tragedy, he lists what families lived in which houses and in many cases the names and ages of the children as well as the occasional bit of family history. It is also known that seventeen men were rescued from the mine and twenty-three from the town.

"The Slide is an unnerving sight, especially at night," Monica explained. "These violent deaths have left an aura over the area. Even in the daylight, it's eerie. Many people report having seen shapes or forms."

With a first-hand viewing of the Frank Slide site, it is impossible not to share that opinion. The horror that was felt that spring night nearly a century ago has left a lasting scar, not only on the landscape but in the ambience of the area under the shadow of Turtle Mountain.

Oddly, the most commonly accepted ghost in the town of Frank has no association with the tragedy of the slide. It is the ghost of Montie Lewis, the local madam. She was known for her great individuality, especially the jewellery she loved and wore constantly, even to bed.

Montie was found murdered one morning, her beloved jewellery missing. Sadly and in typically terror-stricken fashion, a Chinese man was charged with her murder. He denied having any part in the killing but was executed by citizens anxious to see a conclusion to this brutal crime.

Not long after, Montie's sometime-live-in boyfriend confessed to the murder. It is said that to this day you can hear her moans as Montie complains of the injustice surrounding her untimely death.

Monica Field explained that the legend of Montie's ghost has become entrenched in the Frank folklore: "Five or six years ago two young boys foolishly started to climb Turtle Mountain late on a Saturday. It got dark and they were stranded on the east face. They screamed for help but it's said their cries couldn't be heard over Montie's moans."

*　*　*

The town of Frank's neighbour, Bellevue, was hit with disaster in 1910. A spontaneous gas explosion killed thirty young men working in the coal mine. When describing the ominous and oppressive feeling of the area, Monica Field included the Bellevue mine as well.

Four years later, Hillcrest, Alberta, made the front pages of newspapers all over Canada. One hundred and eighty-nine miners lost their lives in Canada's worst single coal-mining disaster.

The mine continued to function as a viable commercial enterprise until 1949, despite a similar occurrence in 1926. Thankfully, only two men were killed that time. A month later, the mine and the miners were working again. It remained an active and profitable coal mine until it was dynamited shut due only to the dwindling demand for coal.

There has been little altered around the Hillcrest Coal Mine. "It hasn't

The mass graves of the victims of the Hillcrest Mine disaster send out a collective agony.

been sanitized at all," explained interpreter Field. "I frequently take groups of school children there. Every time I do, I can feel the presence of those miners and their families. I can feel the men's disbelief and the agony of the families waiting at the entrance to the mine."

Few people can visit the area and come away unmoved. This is one instance where it is unquestioningly the area and not the individual that is haunted.

54: Heavy
with Spirits

Wayne (formerly Rosedeer), Alberta, is a ghost town. How fitting, then, that it is haunted.

Once, it was a bustling metropolis of over 3,000 hard-living souls. Today, Fred Dayman, the owner and operator of the Last Chance Saloon in the Rosedeer Hotel, is one of only a couple of dozen remaining residents. The hotel has been in Fred's family for forty-five years, and he was raised in it. If anyone's in town, whether they're ghostly or warm blooded, it's a fair bet that Fred will know about them.

The Last Chance Saloon is as unique as its proprietor and its ghost-town location. Draft beer is served in jars, and Fred can always be counted on to provide local colour. Although he's never seen the hotel's ghost, he has heard the apparition and felt its presence. As any good inn-keeper would, Fred's also kept careful track of strange reports from his guests over the years.

He took time one summer afternoon to explain the history of the town.

"This was a tough area. It was coal-mining country. There were the workers, the unions, the Communists and the Ku Klux Klan."

Certainly not a situation conducive to building a serene neighbourhood.

In Wayne, Alberta, some patrons of the Last Chance Saloon are familiar with its resident ghost. Other visitors are content to drink draft beer from jam jars.

"In the 1920s the Klan tarred and feathered a fellow up on the third floor. It's been closed off for years now. Even today people don't like to go near it."

It seems, though, that some people just can't leave well enough alone. A woman who was staying in the hotel told Fred she could point out the exact room where the torture took place. She found the ominous atmosphere particularly concentrated around one room.

*   *   *

It's not just the hotel and the bar that are haunted in what remains of Wayne, Alberta.

"The whole area is heavy with spirit," Fred remarked. "There was an Indian camp and graveyard nearby. There have been problems [with ghosts] there too."

Not surprisingly, when the town was in its heyday, there were more demonstrative difficulties. The proximity of the free-living, young coal miners to the exotic Indian maidens created predictable hostilities. The men would slim down their wallets and fatten up their courage at the Last Chance. The Indian men did not take kindly to drunk white men pursuing their women. More than a few miners' bodies were found in Rosebud Creek.

When Fred was a teenager, he and his friends partied regularly in that area. The tradition came to an abrupt halt when one young couple who were parked, no doubt to enjoy the moonlit evening, heard a tremendous thump on the side of their car. They were sufficiently jolted by the noise to stop what they were doing and investigate. There was no one near their car but there were footprints leading to the car door where the thump was heard. No footprints led away from the car.

It was assumed then and continues to be now that the disturbance was caused by either an Indian spirit or that of a coal miner who once caroused too courageously.

*　　*　　*

On the outskirts of town and high up on a hill, there is a graveyard.

"It hasn't been used since 1938," Fred reported.

Is it full then?

"No, there's lots of space left, but there's no road leading up to it. You can't drive there. You have to walk. It was difficult for burials, so people started using the graveyard in Drumheller. Then the town began to die and the old graveyard became abandoned."

That certainly sounds like a perfect scenario for at least one ghost. Although in the last few years a few people have requested that their ashes be scattered around the countryside, no one has gone up to the old cemetery for years. Perhaps those who are resting there do not wish to be disturbed.

55: Prehistoric Beasts Return to Drumheller

The unique landscape of Alberta's badlands around Drumheller is a treasure for scientists. Millions of years ago, the area was a tropical jungle where dinosaurs roamed, feeding on lush vegetation. Apparently, the world's climate cooled, the jungles that had been the food supply for the mammoth reptiles withered, and the huge beasts became extinct. The legacy of both the animal and vegetable life remains in the form of fossils of dinosaur bones and rich coal seams.

For the first fifty years of this century, hard-working miners dug their way underground to exploit these coal reserves. Jake Halliday was one of those miners. For many years, Jake was employed at the Atlas Coal Mine in East Coulee, thirteen miles southeast of Drumheller.

A conscientious employee, Jake soon rose through the ranks to the position of Machine Boss, responsible for repairs to all electrical, mechanical and welding equipment.

On April 10, 1948, Jake had gone down the mine on his day off. There was work that needed to be completed before full production began on Monday morning.

"I remember the date clearly," Jake said. "It was exactly one week before my twenty-sixth birthday. I was doing some welding, but it wasn't progressing as fast as I had hoped. I stopped welding for a moment while I contemplated my next move. The only noise in the mine was the whine of the A.C.-driven arc welder.

"Suddenly, over the noise of the welder, I heard a distant 'thud', then another and another," Jake continued. "It sounded like the footsteps of a heavy animal. I shut down the welder so that I could listen to the noise more clearly. The 'thudding' noise continued and seemed to be getting much closer to the machine shop where I was. That was three miles underground!"

Jake was terrified. Chills ran up his spine and he could feel the hair on the nape of his neck stand on end. When he saw hundreds of mice fleeing toward the entrance, he panicked. Mining lore holds that mice have a sixth sense and can detect impending disaster. When he heard the mine's support timbers creaking and snapping, he fled for his life.

"As I travelled toward the outside I kept turning my head to see if anything was following me out," Jake recalled. "There were only mice. Once I reached the outside, I breathed a lot easier. The nightmare was over."

Amazingly, the next day Jake headed back underground and worked undisturbed until the job was completed.

"I did not mention the incident to anyone," he confirmed.

It was forty years later before he allowed himself to mentally re-live the ghosts of the dinosaurs pounding in the strata above him.

"I was researching my book," he explained. "I came to the location of that mine entrance. It had been dynamited closed. I paused and had many lingering thoughts of the incident that had occurred on April 10, 1948."

56: East Coulee's Resident Who Never Ages

In 1928, East Coulee and the towns surrounding it were booming. The area is rich with coal, and in the early 1900s the fuel was very much in demand. One of the last mines to close was the Atlas Mine. It was still operational less than fifty years ago.

The Atlas Mine was owned and operated by the Patrick family. The business was certainly a successful one but, sadly, the family had experienced a great tragedy. In 1928, when little Billie Patrick was only two years old, he wandered away from his yard where he and his dog had been happily playing. Despite an intensive search, the town's people were not able to find Billie. The poor dog appeared several hours later, soaked to the bone and limping badly. Unfortunately, the bedraggled mutt had no way of communicating his experience with the frantic searchers. The hunt for Billie continued, but no trace of him was ever found. It was generally accepted that he had drowned.

Despite the longevity of the mining operation, the intervening years were not kind to East Coulee. For many years, the place was considered virtually a ghost town, its population had dipped to well below 100. Only recently, some of the long-empty houses have started to fill up again. People are finding that the price of real estate in a ghost town is appealing, and now the population is up to a bustling 250 souls. Or should that be 251?

The house where Billie Patrick lived during his short existence still stands. In the 1980s, it was owned by a family with three children, who "could sense the presence of a small boy. They said that sometimes he would come to play with them," Carol Steward of East Coulee explained.

Whenever the family left the house, the children maintained they could see the boy's image at a window. The little waif would watch the family as they left the house. To reassure the lad, the youngsters took to waving goodbye to him.

The children's parents never saw the child but they did report that they may have heard the pitter patter of footsteps when they knew their own children were in bed and fast asleep.

As a precaution, the mother arranged to have the house exorcised. It's likely that the exorcism was a success, but no one knows for sure because the family moved away not long after the ritual had been performed.

The next family to move into Billie's old house didn't have children, and if they occasionally had a strange visitor they never mentioned it to their friends in the community. Today the house is home to children once again. Carol Steward indicated that the new owners have never mentioned anything out of the ordinary.

Perhaps little Billie Patrick has finally gone to his eternal rest. Or perhaps the new owners' children just aren't ready to share information about their special playmate with anyone as boring as an adult.

57: Medicine Hat's Phantom Train

The story of Medicine Hat's ghost train is deeply ingrained in the city's history. You would be hard pressed to find an adult resident of the southern city who was not well aware of the legend. The tale even rated its own chapter when local historians compiled and published the area's local history.

B ob Twohey and Gus Day worked for the Canadian Pacific Railway, Bob as an engineer and Gus as a fireman. On a fine June morning in 1908, the two men were busy with their duties as the train they were operating made its way from Medicine Hat to Dunmore.

Suddenly, another train appeared. It was approaching theirs. The two trains were travelling on the single track in opposite directions, and there could only be one result. Engineer Twohey made for the gangplank to jump to safety, and he called to his partner to do the same.

In a final attempt to avert disaster, Fireman Day grabbed for the brake handle before joining Twohey. The approaching train sounded a warning whistle, and both men stood frozen in fear. With eyes like saucers, the railway men watched in disbelief as their engine passed the second train.

"The coach windows were lighted, and crew members waved a greeting from places where crew members would be expected to be found waving greetings as trains pass one another," Day reported.

The inevitable head-on crash never occurred. The approaching train had not, after all, been travelling on the same track as Day and Twohey's. It had sped smoothly along beside the scheduled one, on nonexistent tracks!

Day and Twohey were badly shaken by the incident. By silent agreement, neither man spoke of the terrifying sighting. A full two weeks passed before they dared mention it, even to one another. Once they had, though, both were somewhat relieved. At least each knew their own mind had not concocted the apparition.

Prior to seeing the phantom train, Bob Twohey had visited a fortune teller. She'd indicated that, despite his current good health, within a month he'd be dead. The man put the two incidents together and wisely decided to take some time off work.

An engineer named J. Nicholson took Twohey's place as Gus Day's partner. All went well for several days. The ghost train memory was beginning to fade in Day's mind until, at exactly the same spot they'd "passed" the mystery train earlier in the month, Day heard his new workmate exclaim, "What the hell's THAT?"

The terrified men stared intently at the train hurtling toward them on their track. Seconds before the inevitable crash occurred the other train veered slightly. With its whistle sounding and headlight beaming, the phantom train once again passed safely beside the scheduled one. In keeping with railway courtesy, the crew members of the second train waved greetings to Nicholson and Day. Nothing seemed out of the ordinary to that crew, despite the fact their train was gliding along nonexistent tracks.

Gus Day reported for his shift on July 8, 1908. He was assigned to yard duty. The position of Fireman on the route to Dunmore was taken by a man named Thompson. The Engineer for the trip was J. Nicholson. They were to pick up the Spokane Flyer at Dunmore and take it further east to Swift Current, Saskatchewan.

As the train Nicholson and Thompson were charged with operating made its way along the route, it inevitably came to the spot where the phantom train had been seen. Again, an oncoming train was sighted. This time it was real. Passenger train 514 from Lethbridge was heading toward the eastbound freight.

Thompson jumped clear moments before the grinding collision. He was the only crew member to survive. Passenger-train crewmen Gray and Mallet as well as seven passengers were killed on the westbound train as was Thompson's partner, Nicholson.

In an investigation after the crash, Thompson recalled seeing a farmer standing on a hill waving frantically. At the time, the crews interpreted the wave only as a friendly greeting. In fact, it was intended as a warning. From his perch, the man had a clear view of the impending disaster.

What a tragedy that neither the farmer's warning nor that of the phantom train had been understood. After all, both engineers had seen both warnings. The engineer of the westbound train that fateful morning was Bob Twohey.

58: Museum Inherits More Than a Building

There's not much question that the Galt Museum in Leth-bridge is haunted. There's also not much question about who the resident ghost is.

"This building was originally a hospital, so many people have died here," explained Richard Shockley, Collection Technician at the Galt Museum. "We presume the ghost is George because his death was accidental."

The incidents surrounding the poor man's death are well documented. On Thursday, February 16, 1933, George Benjamin Bailey was admitted to the hospital in preparation for some minor surgery. As he was being taken from the main floor up to the operating room, a tragic accident occurred. The gurney Bailey was lying on was pushed partly into the elevator, and then for no apparent reason, the lift began to move up. George's wife, Alice, watched in horror as half of the rolling stretcher rode up in the elevator. Inevitably, the gurney tipped. George Bailey slipped off and fell fifteen feet to the bottom of the elevator shaft. He suffered severe head injuries and died later that evening.

The next day, the newspapers were filled with the story. The victim of this bizarre accident had been a prominent farmer from a nearby village. His widow sued the hospital who, in turn, sued the elevator company. Interestingly, the same lawyer represented both Mrs. Bailey and the hos-

The Galt Museum in Lethbridge is home to a ghost whose human form was killed in a freak accident.

pital. It's doubtful that such a situation would be tolerated today. Despite this apparent conflict of interest, it is reported by a relative that Alice Bailey received, in compensation for her husband's accidental death, the princely sum of $40 per month until her own death thirteen years later.

When Mrs. Bailey died, one can only hope that she had not looked forward to a reunion with her husband. It would seem that George, understandably, feels he has some unfinished business at the scene of his untimely death.

In the fall of 1985, work to convert the old building into the city's museum was nearly completed. Authorities wanted someone in the building as much as possible during this period and, as a result, Richard Shockley worked some very long hours.

"I was here almost twenty-four hours a day. It was then that I had my experiences with George. When I was working at my desk in the basement work area, I heard a rustling or shuffling sound from the hallway. It reminded me of the sound my grandfather used to make as he shuffled along the floor in his slippers. The noise would always stop when it got to my office door. Initially, of course, I presumed it was just building noises, but they were too consistent and frequent. Also, I definitely felt a presence, a strong sense of someone being there. Then I heard the same shuffling noise, this time going away."

The second time Richard had this experience, he was a little better prepared. As he heard the sounds receding back down the hallway, he quietly moved from his desk to look down the hall. "I saw a soft white light (between a double set of windowed doors) move from west to east. It couldn't have been a reflection. It moved slowly. I opened the locked door and immediately sensed something in there. It was cold, clammy, and musty – unnerving but not frightening. It had to be a ghost."

Richard discovered that the area of the basement where he'd seen the strange light and then felt the unusual presence had been between the morgue and the autopsy room. A likely "haunt" for George considering the circumstances of his death.

Richard isn't the only one with tales of George, but not everyone is interested in talking about their experiences.

An employee with the telephone company recently declined an invitation to speak at the Galt Museum's annual Hallowe'en presentation. Lorraine Page of the museum explained that when she asked him to share his experience, the man was adamant that he didn't want to talk about it.

"He said even thinking about it still upsets him and talking about it causes him to lose sleep."

In order to protect the man's serenity we'll refer to him only as "Frank."

Frank's experience with the ghost of the Galt Museum goes back to the 1970s, when the building served as a local health unit. He and his coworker were the only two people in the building. They were working to run lines from the basement to the main floor. Frank was in the basement when the ladder he was standing on began to shake. At the same time, despite the summer heat, a blast of cold air came out of nowhere.

Presuming his partner was right beside him and responsible for the annoying incidents, Frank told him to stop. His reply came in the form of a disembodied voice from the first floor assuring him his partner was up there and not able to hear Frank's voice clearly enough to make out what he'd been saying. The poor man has never forgotten the unsettling experience.

Other museum employees report hearing doors slam when they know there's no one in that particular section of the building.

Cecile McCleary, curator at the museum, added, "We frequently smell food around here when there is none."

Could George be cooking up the post-surgery meal he would have missed? Of course, we'll never know because George seems content to stay in the realm in which he died: he's never ventured into the impressive new addition now attached to the building he died in.

"No one's ever had a strange experience anywhere but in the old section, the part that was the hospital and only in the basement or on the first floor," Cecile explained.

Lorraine Page, whose job it is to organize the evening of ghost stories around Hallowe'en, chuckled as she said, "After the stories have all been told, we always lead the audience on a darkened tour of the basement hallways!"

To date, George has not joined the tour. Perhaps this year ...

59: Was it Star?

The Bowman School in Lethbridge was built over a hundred years ago. Today, the stately building has been extensively refurbished and is known as the Bowman Arts Centre.

Nearly twenty years ago, writer Joan Waterfield heard heart-wrenching sobbing, and when recently reminded of it, the depth of emotion she had experienced then was still evident.

"It was in the old loos," Joan explained, revealing her British background. "The washrooms have been changed since then but at that time the girls' room was upstairs. Occasionally, one of the children from the ballet school would become upset, and I would take her into my office and comfort her until her parents arrived."

This is what Joan expected had happened when she heard the forlorn weeping.

"I followed the sound to the girls' washroom, but there was no one there. It was not only the crying," Joan continued. "But there was a definite feeling of a presence. I could feel the child's great need and terrible unhappiness."

Confused, Joan searched the building for the obviously distressed child. The unnerving incident recurred and yet no child was ever found when the sobbing was heard.

Lethbridge's Bowman Arts Centre (formerly Bowman School) was the source of a child's pitiful cries, years after they had occurred.

"I began to think of the child as 'The Sad Little One'. Later, when I heard the sobbing, I would call to her and try to comfort her. I would say, 'it's all right, Star, it's only me'."

"Star?" I asked. "Where did the name come from?"

"That's Carol Watkinson's story."

Carol, who was the executive secretary at the Centre, reacted to my question with a prolonged chuckle: "Not this again! I've told this story so many times!"

When she was assured there was only one question involved, Carol readily supplied the explanation.

"I was speaking with a friend about the sobbing sounds. He'd been raised in Lethbridge, and as soon as he heard my description he said, 'that's Star'."

More than fifty years before Carol and Joan heard the unexplained sobbing and when Carol's friend was just a youngster, he remembered a little Chinese girl named Star. She dressed in the traditional Chinese fashion of the era. This included trousers. Star was entering the girls' washroom when a teacher spotted her. Because of the clothing, the teacher mistook Star for a boy and beat her. The child, understandably, sobbed for days after, Carol's friend recalled.

It was the child's horror at the abuse that both Carol and Joan had heard and felt.

"We're both very practical, reality-rooted people," explained Joan. "But we both felt it so deeply."

Carol added, "I'm a sceptic, myself, but it was a very moving experience."

Since the ladies' experiences, the Bowman Arts Centre has been renovated and the washrooms moved and modernized. The pathetic, sobbing sounds are no longer experienced.

Just one further note to this melancholy tale. The waif who was Star grew up and moved to Vancouver. Star was still very much alive when her ghostly sobbing was heard.

60: Building Demolished, Ghost Remains

Lethbridge's Marquis Hotel was torn down after a full, sixty-year life. The building's been gone for almost five years now, so it's unlikely that the mystery of Mathilda will ever be solved.

Our story begins in 1931, when Room 327 was rented out to a man and a woman. Some say the woman was a native; others say that's not so. All agree, though, that no one checked out of that room the following day.

When housekeepers arrived the next morning to give the room a routine cleaning, what they found was anything but routine. The empty room was a blood-splattered mess. No one was ever able to find out what had happened on that fateful night.

Not long after the gruesome incident, an unfortunate traveller checked into the Marquis and Room 327. In the middle of the night, the man awoke to the feeling of being watched – a native woman was staring intently at him. Terrified, he grabbed his suitcase, fled the room, and got on the elevator. Unfortunately, the first glance he took around the elevator he thought he was riding to safety revealed the native woman right beside him, still staring.

The night clerk could hear the frightened man's screams as the elevator descended to the main floor. The clerk armed himself with a baseball bat and waited for the sliding doors to open. When they did, only the horrified man emerged.

After that incident, Room 327 was not rented out, and it remained empty until a member of the Marquis staff stayed in it. She only lasted a portion of the night, fleeing when she felt someone watching her in the shower.

Psychics frequently reported that there was definitely something in that room. Some said it was apparent as soon as you neared the door. The ravaged and distraught presence became accepted by the hotel staff and was even given a name: Mathilda.

She was also credited with flicking on and off lights in and around the basement of the Marquis. It is suspected, too, that Mathilda had a hand in the occasionally strange behaviour of the hotel's elevator.

The hotel was the first building in Lethbridge to have an elevator. Its doors could only be opened from the inside and yet, on a few occasions, it was witnessed descending from the third floor to the main floor where the door would open, seemingly of its own accord, to reveal an empty elevator. A mere malfunction? Possibly, except the night watchman who observed the phenomenon reported that his guard dog ran to the opening door, barking excitedly, wagging his tail, and looking expectantly into the empty lift.

Before the Marquis was torn down, some members of the Lethbridge media decided to make one last attempt to solve the mystery. They stayed the night in the old, deserted hotel. Unfortunately, they didn't get to meet Mathilda. Several pieces of their equipment malfunctioned for no apparent reason, but other than that, the night was uncomfortable but without incident.

The Marquis is gone now and she has taken her secrets with her.

61: Rented House With Unwanted Options

In May of 1981, Jane Mauthe was a young bride. A coworker of her husband's made the couple an interesting offer shortly after the wedding. He had purchased a large and luxurious home in a comfortable corner of Lethbridge but was not ready to move into it yet himself. Would they like to rent the home from him at a very reasonable rate? Not surprisingly, the Mauthes happily took the man up on his offer.

"When my husband's friend bought the home in 1981, he paid $114,000 for it, so you can imagine that it was quite a nice place. The man really wanted to own the house, but he was still single and living with his parents," Jane explained.

The house was almost new. There'd only been one former occupant, a business couple. The wife had owned a successful bath boutique in the city. Sadly, she had recently died, of an apparent aneurysm, while working in the kitchen.

"The first strange thing we noticed was in the master bedroom. A painting that had been a wedding present kept falling off the wall. This happened about six times. We'd come home and find it on the floor. Without thinking too much about it, we just put it back up on the wall. Finally, after it had fallen about six times, we came home and found it on the floor, smashed."

The bathroom off the master bedroom had a sunken marble bathtub. Sounds like everyone's ideal for relaxing in before bed, doesn't it? Not so.

"I never felt comfortable in the ensuite bathroom. Especially in the bathtub. Actually, we rarely used it. It always felt cold and clammy in there and there was a draft from somewhere. We could never detect where it came from, though," Jane said. "The water in the tub would sometimes turn on for no reason. That was a little unsettling. We phoned my husband's friend, our landlord, and he had it checked out, but no one could ever find a reason why the taps would do that."

The "problems" continued to the main bathroom.

"The toilet in there kept flushing, even when no one was in the room. The landlord also had that checked but no explanation was ever given and it continued.

Another puzzling feature of their real-estate bargain was an area of damp-feeling air in the master bedroom. Downstairs, the entire room Jane's husband used as his den was constantly dark and cold.

"It was terribly drafty. We found out later that it had been the lady's sewing room," Jane continued.

The house had a formal dining room. It could be separated from the rest of the house by a pocket door. Periodically, the door would slide closed and then open again. Upon investigation, Jane discovered that the former lady of the house had loved to entertain. Perhaps this is what she was doing when the door would move of its own accord.

When Jane and her husband had entertained, the resident spirit clearly wanted the guests to stay.

"We gave a dinner party one evening and this lady didn't want our company to leave. The first thing she did was smash the glass bowl the salad was in. It had been a wedding gift and that was the first time I'd ever used it. The bowl was just sitting on the table and suddenly it shattered."

Once the apparition had everyone's attention, she continued her hijinks.

"Later that evening she wouldn't let the guests leave. We tried several doors and couldn't get any of them to open. As a last resort, we went through the attached garage and tried to open the garage doors manually. They wouldn't budge either."

Jane's visitors must share her calm nature because their response was to enjoy their hosts' hospitality for another few hours before trying to leave a second time. The front and back doors still would not unlock, but they were able to open a garage door.

"We had a locksmith come in and he could find no reason for the doors not opening," Jane recalled.

Within a year the young couple had purchased their own home and moved out.

"We sublet it to three roommates. They stayed in the house for two years. I spoke to one of the young women and she said the wall-to-wall mirror in the master bedroom had smashed on more than one occasion, never when anyone was home."

Shortly after they moved out, the owner sold the house, never having lived in it himself.

"We were out for a drive recently and passed the house. We explained to our daughters that that was where we'd lived when we were first married," Jane recalled.

"It looked very well cared for. The lawns were nicely kept. I was glad to see that," the former tenant conceded.

Perhaps the original owner wasn't keen on having people staying in her beloved home unless they were planning to settle there. Hopefully, both she and the current occupants are happy with the present situation.

62: Keeping Watch

Kilmorey Lodge is nestled inside the gates of beautiful Waterton Park. Leslie Muza, owner of the lodge, is a warm and welcoming woman who thoroughly enjoys her niche in the area's tourist trade. Her extensive knowledge of local history, and particularly the history of Kilmorey Lodge itself, is a bonus for guests. Without too much prompting, Leslie may even entertain you with stories of their resident ghost.

"We call her Mrs. Kilmorey," Leslie explained in a matter of fact way. "We don't know exactly who she is – was? Possibly she's one of the former owners of the place."

Leslie's never seen Mrs. Kilmorey, but she's felt her presence many times. She's even witnessed some of the apparition's high jinks.

"This is a very old building, and repairs and renovations are a frequent necessity," the proprietor explained.

Over the years, and as the building's use and owners changed, there have been major alterations.

"This is our sixth season with the lodge and I can tell you Mrs. Kilmorey doesn't like the renovations. They really upset her and she becomes quite active."

Over the years, the lady has frequently been known to cause lights to turn on and off, swinging doors open and close, apparently of their own

In Waterton Park, a spirit sits by the front door of Kilmorey Lodge, keeping watch.

volition, and other doors to slam closed for no apparent reason. Leslie chuckled as she recalled a slightly off-the-wall stunt the ghost pulled.

"Potatoes. She'd piled all the potatoes in the middle of the kitchen floor."

Leslie is not the only brunt of the lady's tricks.

"One morning, our waitress supervisor was preparing the first pot of breakfast coffee for our guests. She went to set the pot on the element and it flew across the room. She was annoyed at first because she assumed the coffee machine's element had been left on all night and the cold pot's contact with the hot surface had caused the accident. Not so. The element was turned off. The surface was not even warm, let alone hot."

Occasionally, guests will tell Leslie that they've felt a woman's presence.

"One couple were visiting from Los Angeles. In the morning the man told me he'd had a sensation of a woman leaning over the bed staring at him. He said it wasn't a frightening or uncomfortable experience at all, just an awareness."

"Several years ago we had a guest who was apparently psychic. As soon as she walked in, she said to me, 'Do you know this building is home to a spirit?'"

It was information from this sensitive visitor that confirmed much of what Leslie had long suspected about their supernatural boarder.

"She assured me that the ghost had a passive nature and was, indeed, a female, an older woman. You know, I'm not sure to this day whether the psychic actually saw her or just felt a suggestion of her."

Whichever it was, the description the psychic guest gave was detailed: a passive spirit of a white-haired woman in her sixties or seventies, wearing a blue floral dress.

"Apparently she has a chair by the front door."

These bits of information were all additional indications to Leslie about the woman's identity.

She continued: "In the early days of the lodge, a woman owned and ran the place by herself. I gather from what I've read and heard over the years that the men in the area gave her a pretty rough time. The industry here is strictly tourism and it can be very competitive. I talked to a man who had boarded with her when he was a youth. He said she was a good business woman who was just keeping her ground. I'm sure there's more to the story than we will ever know. You're dealing with the dynamics of business people in a small community."

Perhaps Mrs. Kilmorey will eventually accept the inevitable and ongoing renovations at Kilmorey Lodge. If she does, she might perhaps enjoy just sitting, forever, in her blue floral print dress by the front door and keeping a kindly watch over Kilmorey Lodge's current owners and guests.